ROCK ART

CDs, ALBUMS & POSTERS

by

SPENCER DRATE

foreword by

ROGER DEAN

PBC

D1454075

An Imprint of

PBC International, Inc.

Distributor to the book trade in the United States and Canada:

Rizzoli International Publications Inc.
300 Park Avenue South
New York, NY 10010

Distributor to the art trade in the United States and Canada:

PBC International, Inc.
One School Street
Glen Cove, NY 11542
1-800-527-2826
Within New York State
call 516-676-2727
Fax 516-676-2738

Distributor throughout the rest of the world:

Hearst Books International
1350 Avenue of the Americas
New York, NY 10019

Library of Congress Cataloging-in-Publication Data

Drate, Spencer.
     Designing for music   /   by Spencer Drate.
          p.   cm.
     Includes index.
     ISBN 0-86636-183-9   ISBN 0-86636-277-0 (pbk)
     1. Sound recordings—Album covers—United States. 2. Music trade—United
States—Marketing. I. Title: Rock Art
     NC1833.U6D7 1992
     741.6'6--dc20   92-11441
                                      CIP

CAVEAT—Information in this text is believed accurate, and will pose no problem
for the student or casual reader. However, the author was often constrained by
information contained in signed release forms, information that could have been in
error or not included at all. Any misinformation (or lack of information) is the result
of failure in these attestations. The author has done whatever is possible to insure
accuracy.

Color separation, printing and binding by
Toppan Printing Co.

Printed in Hong Kong

Typography by
TypeLink, Inc.

10 9 8 7 6 5 4 3 2 1

BOOK DESIGN BY JÜTKA SALAVETZ (MOM)

THIS BOOK IS DEDICATED TO JUSTIN AND ARIEL

THROUGH MY CAREER TO THE EVOLUTION OF THIS BOOK—VERY SPECIAL

THANKS TO: JÜTKA, JUSTIN AND ARIEL (MY INSPIRATION), KEVIN CLARK, MARK

SERCHUCK AND EVERYONE AT PBC, ROGER DEAN (THE GUIDING LIGHT),

STORM, MICHAEL BAYS, JERI HEIDEN, JEFF GOLD AND ALL AT WARNER BROS.

RECORDS, VAUGHAN OLIVER, TOMMY STEELE, ALL THE DESIGNERS AND

PHOTOGRAPHERS PARTICIPATING, SEYMOUR STEIN, BERNARD STOLLMAN,

HOWARD AND GERRY AT EVIDENCE MUSIC, LOU AND SYLVIA REED, KENNY AND

MERYL LAGUNA, AND JOAN JETT, MTV, ANNIE LIEBOVITZ, STEVE KARAS, ALL

THE WRITERS AND THE MEDIA THAT HAVE INTERVIEWED ME, TONY WRIGHT,

GEORGE DUBOSE, MAUREEN HINDIN, PAT BARRY AND ALL AT ISLAND RECORDS,

U2, BOB ANTLER AND SALLIE BALDWIN, PAT KENNY, THE SPIRITS OF RICK

ACKNOWLEDGMENTS

GRIFFIN AND BARNEY BUBBLES, THE FIRST LED ZEPPELIN LP COVER, SOUNDS,

SMASH COMPACT DISCS, ALL THE RECORDING ARTISTS THAT I HAVE DESIGNED

FOR, RICHARD ROTH, LAURI GOLDSTEIN AND ALL AT NARAS NYC, RON

ALEXENBURG, WARING ABBOTT, ZORAN BUSIC, MICHAEL PILLOT, MICHAEL

LEMBO, ARTHUR MANN, PETER GIDION, MARK PROCT, DAN BECK, ROBERT

SMITH, JOHN GILLESPIE, TONY SCHAEFFER, CHRISTOPHER WALKER AND BILL

DOBLE AND CABIN FEVER MUSIC, GARY F. MONTGOMERY, MARTIN FOLKMAN,

BAN THE BOX, AND ALL THE MANY OTHER PEOPLE THAT HAVE HELPED MAKE

MY CAREER SUCCESSFUL.

HISTORICALLY, GRAPHIC DESIGN HAS A STIGMA ATTACHED TO ITS

TITLE; IT HAS NEVER ATTAINED THE QUALITY OF RESPECT THAT IS

ATTRIBUTED TO "FINE ART."

I SEE THE WORLD OF MUSIC FROM A "FINE ART" POINT OF VIEW—

THE MUSIC IS THE MOTHER IN ME AND ART OR DESIGN IS THE

FATHER. THIS INCREDIBLE MEETING OF MUSIC AND ART HAS BEEN

THE DRIVING FORCE BEHIND THE PATH I HAVE CHOSEN IN LIFE. I

HAVE BEEN LUCKY ENOUGH TO MAKE A CAREER OUT OF THIS

SPECIAL RELATIONSHIP, BUT I ALSO FEEL THAT THE BEAUTY

CREATED BY MIXING MUSIC AND ART SHOULD BE SHARED SO THAT

ALL CAN ENJOY AND PERHAPS GAIN INSPIRATION FROM IT.

INTRODUCTION

THIS BOOK IS A SMALL SAMPLE OF GRAPHIC DESIGNERS WHO HAVE

SHARED IN THAT SPECIAL RELATIONSHIP WITH MUSIC.

LISTEN TO THE ART

SPENCER DRATE

CONTENTS

THIS BOOK IS ABOUT THE WORK OF ARTISTS AND DESIGNERS WHO HAVE EXPLORED THE COASTLINE OR MARGIN WHERE MUSIC AND ART MEET.

FOR THE PAST 23 YEARS, THIS EDGE HAS NOT ONLY FASCINATED ME AS AN OBSERVER, BUT HAS ALSO ENTICED AND ABSORBED ME AS AN ARTIST. I NEVER BELIEVED THAT IT WAS POSSIBLE FOR A MUSICIAN TO 'CONJURE UP' AN IMAGE. CAN YOU IMAGINE AN ARTIST SAYING TO BEETHOVEN: "YES, IT'S GREAT AS FAR AS IT GOES, BUT I THINK YOU'VE GOT THE TREES IN THE WRONG PLACE"? IT WILL NOT DO—IT CAN'T BE DONE; AND EVEN IF IT COULD, I SUSPECT IT WOULD BE REDUNDANT AND ALTOGETHER LESS INTERESTING ANYWAY. HOWEVER, SOMETHING DOES HAPPEN WHEN ART AND MUSIC COME TOGETHER: EACH HAS AN EFFECT ON THE OTHER, A REACTION IS PRODUCED.

A PARTICULAR PIECE OF MUSIC CAN ALTER THE WAY IN WHICH ONE SEES A CERTAIN IMAGE, AND DIFFERENT MUSIC WILL PRODUCE YET MORE CHANGES IN THAT PERCEPTION. MORE PERTINENTLY, WITH THIS BOOK IN MIND, THE OPPOSITE IS ALSO TRUE— OBVIOUS PERHAPS, BUT STILL INTERESTING.

THIS BOUNDARY POSES A CHALLENGE TO BOTH ARTISTS AND MUSICIANS ALIKE. IT IS A CREATIVE FURNACE WHERE NEW HERALDRY, NEW ICONS, AND EVEN NEW LANGUAGES ARE FORMED IN A CONSTANTLY CHANGING FERMENT OF IMAGE AND INVENTION.

I WAS SHOCKED INTO AWARENESS OF THE INCREDIBLE POTENTIAL OF THIS

BY SEEING RICK GRIFFIN'S 'AOXOMOXOA.' IT WAS 1969, AND I WAS LIVING IN LONDON, JUST OUT OF COLLEGE, BROKE AND MORE TO THE POINT, HAD NO HI FI. OUT WALKING, I CAUGHT A GLIMPSE OF RICK GRIFFIN'S DESIGN FOR 'AOXOMOXOA.' IT STRUCK ME AS STUNNING, ALIEN, BEAUTIFUL AND COMPLETE; HAVING THE INTEGRITY OF AN ARTIFACT FROM AN ANCIENT, LONG-ESTABLISHED BUT ENTIRELY 'OTHER' CULTURE. I WAS FASCINATED BY THE DESIGN, AND WALKING AWAY SEVERAL TIMES BEFORE RETURNING TO BUY WHAT WAS NOT ONLY THE FIRST ALBUM I BOUGHT FOR ITS COVER, BUT ALSO THE FIRST ALBUM I EVER BOUGHT. I STILL LOVE IT.

THIS EXPERIENCE INSPIRED ME TO START COLLECTING ALBUMS FOR THEIR COVERS—WHICH I STILL DO.

FOREWORD

SEVEN YEARS LATER, IN 1976, WHEN STORM THORGERSON (HIPGNOSIS) AND I COMPILED AND EDITED THE FIRST ALBUM COVER ALBUM WE PUT 'AOXOMOXOA' ON THE FRONT COVER. THE STRANGENESS AND INCREDIBLE ORIGINALITY OF IT IS THE FIRST AND LASTING IMPRESSION ONE GETS OF THE 'AOXOMOXOA' COVER DESIGN. THIS EFFECT COMES NOT SO MUCH FROM THE SUBJECT MATTER, OR EVEN FROM HIS WONDERFULLY IDIOSYNCRATIC STYLE, BUT COMES I BELIEVE, FROM THE LETTERING. THE MOST ORDINARY AND EVERYDAY THINGS WILL BE, OR APPEAR, WONDERFUL AND EXOTIC IF THEY COME FROM WONDERFUL AND EXOTIC PLACES. A CAN OF COOKING OIL FROM TIBET WILL BE MORE EXCITING THAN THE SAME ITEM FROM THE LOCAL SUPERMARKET. IT IS THE LETTERING WHICH FIRST SIGNALS

AND EVOKES THE STRANGE AND EXOTIC NATURE OF THE THING.

SO, HOW MUCH MORE EXOTIC, HOW MUCH MORE FOREIGN WAS THAT MYSTERIOUS CULTURE FROM WHENCE CAME RICK GRIFFIN'S ART? HIS MARK WAS SO SURE, HIS TYPOGRAPHIC INTUITION SO SHREWD, THAT HE COULD PRODUCE TYPE, CONVENTIONALLY MEANINGLESS, THAT STILL CONVEYED THE MESSAGE WITH ABSOLUTE PRECISION. THE MESSAGE WAS USUALLY: "FOR YOUR EDIFICATION, PLEASURE OR ENLIGHTENMENT — LOOK AGAIN." IT WORKED EXTRAORDINARILY WELL SYMBOLICALLY AND ICONOGRAPHICALLY. BUT WHAT OF THE MUSIC OF THE 'GRATEFUL DEAD'? WAS IT AS AMAZING AND STRANGE AS THE COVER — DID IT COME FROM THAT 'OTHER' CULTURE? PERHAPS; IT WAS GOOD — BUT I THINK THEY OWE A KELLY, WHO WERE ALSO KEY TO BUILDING THAT PARTICULAR LEGEND.

1969 WAS AN INTERESTING YEAR. I HAD, ALMOST BY ACCIDENT PAINTED MY FIRST ALBUM COVER, AND I WAS LIVING IN THE SAME BUILDING AS STORM, WHERE HE AND PO WERE SETTING UP HIPGNOSIS. THROUGHOUT THE '70S, THEY PRODUCED SLEEVES DOMINATED BY IMAGES THAT WERE EXTRAORDINARILY BEAUTIFUL, HUMOROUS AND SURREAL. MORE RECENTLY, I HAVE WORKED WITH VAUGHAN OLIVER WHO SEEMS TO BE ABLE TO ABANDON IMAGE, TO BE ABLE TO WORK WITH THE MOST SIMPLE AND ORDINARY TYPE, AND STILL TO PRODUCE WORKS OF WONDER. HE DOES HOWEVER OCCASIONALLY WORK WITH CALLIGRAPHER CHRIS BIGG WHO, WHILST HIS WORK IS TOTALLY UNLIKE RICK GRIFFIN'S, CAN MAKE SEEMINGLY MEANINGLESS MARKS ON PAPER WORK TO THE SAME EXTRAORDINARY EFFECT.

THE RELATIONSHIP BETWEEN ART AND MUSIC IS FOR ME HOWEVER, STILL MYSTERIOUS; FASCINATING BUT FUGITIVE. THE BAND CAN SIMPLY BE PICTURED, THE WORDS CAN BE INTERPRETED, OR AMBIENT ICONS INCORPORATED, STREET HERALDRY INVENTED, THE PAST PLUNDERED AND THE FUTURE PLANNED — IN FACT, ALMOST ANYTHING. STRANGELY, IT ALL SEEMS TO WORK, AND SOME OF THE MOST INTERESTING ART OF OUR TIME HAS COME FROM THIS UNEASY SYMBIOSIS. IN THE SUMMER OF 1991 RICK GRIFFIN DIED: A PERSONAL AND CULTURAL TRAGEDY. AT THE TIME I WROTE ABOUT HIM, AND IN THIS INTRODUCTION I BORROWED A LITTLE FROM THAT PIECE.

ROGER DEAN, 1992

MARTYN ATKINS

BORN IN HUDDERSFIELD, ENGLAND IN 1958, MARTYN ATTENDED HALIFAX AND BRADFORD'S ART SCHOOLS AND EVENTUALLY MAJORED IN GRAPHIC DESIGN.

IN 1980, MARTYN DESIGNED JACKETS FOR ALTERNATIVE BANDS SUCH AS A CERTAIN RATIO, SECTION 25 AND JOY DIVISION. IN 1981, MARTYN'S DESIGN FOR THE ECHO AND THE BUNNYMEN ALBUM "HEAVEN UP HERE" WON THE NEW MUSICAL EXPRESS ALBUM COVER OF THE YEAR AWARD. THROUGHOUT THE '80S, HE LECTURED ON HIS WORK AT LEADING BRITISH ART SCHOOLS.

HE SET UP HIS OWN DESIGN COMPANY, TOWN & COUNTRY PLANNING (T&CP), AND HAS WORKED CLOSELY WITH DEPECHE MODE CREATING MANY OF THEIR DESIGN/ADVERTISING CAMPAIGNS INCLUDING THE AWARD-WINNING ALBUM COVER FOR "A BROKEN FRAME." MORE RECENTLY, MARTYN HAS DIRECTED MUSIC VIDEOS FOR ARTISTS IN BOTH AMERICA AND EUROPE, INCLUDING DEPECHE MODE.

PERFORMING ARTIST
DEPECHE MODE
ALBUM TITLE
A BROKEN FRAME
DESIGNER AND ART DIRECTOR
MARTYN ATKINS (T + CP ASSOC.)
CALLIGRAPHY
CHING CHING LEE
RECORD COMPANY
MUTE RECORDS ©
PHOTOGRAPHER
BRIAN GRIFFIN

PHOTO: CHRIS KEMP

PERFORMING ARTIST
DEPECHE MODE
ALBUM TITLE
STRANGELOVE (12" LIMITED EDITION SINGLE)
DESIGNERS
**MARTYN ATKINS, MARK HIGENBOTTAM
AND DAVID JONES (T + CP ASSOC.)**

ART DIRECTOR
MARTYN ATKINS
RECORD COMPANY
MUTE RECORDS ©
PHOTOGRAPHER
MARTYN ATKINS

PERFORMING ARTIST
DEPECHE MODE
ALBUM TITLE
NEVER LET ME DOWN
DESIGNERS
**MARTYN ATKINS, MARK HIGENBOTTAM
AND DAVID JONES (T + CP ASSOC.)**

ART DIRECTOR
MARTYN ATKINS
RECORD COMPANY
MUTE RECORDS ©
PHOTOGRAPHER
MARTYN ATKINS

PERFORMING ARTIST
DEPECHE MODE
ALBUM TITLE
BEHIND THE WHEEL (7" & 12" SINGLE)

DESIGNERS
**MARTYN ATKINS
MARK HIGENBOTTAM AND DAVID JONES
(T + CP ASSOC.)**
RECORD COMPANY
MUTE RECORDS ©

PERFORMING ARTIST
DEPECHE MODE
ALBUM TITLE
MUSIC FOR THE MASSES
DESIGNERS
**MARTYN ATKINS, MARK HIGENBOTTAM
AND DAVID JONES (T + CP ASSOC.)**
ART DIRECTOR
MARTYN ATKINS
RECORD COMPANY
MUTE RECORDS ©
PHOTOGRAPHER
MARTYN ATKINS

PERFORMING ARTIST
DEPECHE MODE
ALBUM TITLE
STRANGELOVE (7" SINGLE)
DESIGNERS
**MARTYN ATKINS, MARK HIGENBOTTAM
AND DAVID JONES (T + CP ASSOC.)**
ART DIRECTOR
MARTYN ATKINS
RECORD COMPANY
MUTE RECORDS ©
PHOTOGRAPHER
MARTYN ATKINS

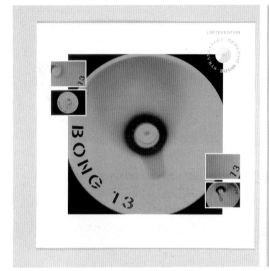

PERFORMING ARTIST
DEPECHE MODE
ALBUM TITLE
X¹ AND X²
DESIGNER
MARTYN ATKINS (T + CP ASSOC.)
RECORD COMPANY
MUTE RECORDS ©
PHOTOGRAPHER
MARTYN ATKINS ASSISTED BY CHRISTOPHER KEMP

CHRISTOPHER AUSTOPCHUK

CHRISTOPHER AUSTOPCHUK, DESIGN DIRECTOR OF SONY MUSIC, HAS BEEN IN THE MUSIC INDUSTRY FOR 12 YEARS. HE HAS CREDITS THAT INCLUDE WORK FOR MCGRAW – HILL, SCHOLASTIC PUBLICATIONS, PUSH PIN STUDIOS, *ROLLING STONE* MAGAZINE, *PARADE* MAGAZINE AND CONDE NAST PUBLICATIONS. HE HAS EARNED OVER 300 AWARDS FROM VARIOUS PROFESSIONAL SOCIETIES AND PUBLICATIONS, AMONG WHICH ARE THE NEW YORK ART DIRECTORS CLUB, PRINT, GRAPHIS, SOCIETY OF PUBLICATION DESIGNERS, AIGA AND CA.

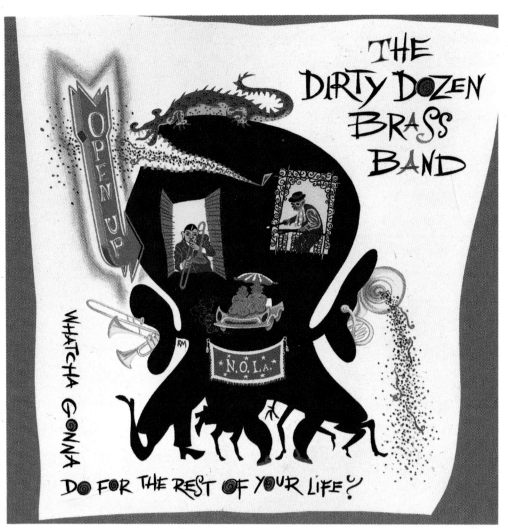

PERFORMING ARTIST
THE DIRTY DOZEN BRASS BAND
ALBUM TITLE
WHATCHA GONNA DO FOR THE REST OF YOUR LIFE?
ART DIRECTOR
CHRISTOPHER AUSTOPCHUK
ILLUSTRATOR
RUTH MARTEN
RECORD COMPANY
© COLUMBIA RECORDS

PERFORMING ARTIST
THE DIRTY DOZEN BRASS BAND
ALBUM TITLE
THE NEW ORLEANS ALBUM
ART DIRECTOR
CHRISTOPHER AUSTOPCHUK
ILLUSTRATOR
JOSH GOSFIELD
RECORD COMPANY
© COLUMBIA RECORDS

15

CHRISTOPHER AUSTOPCHUK

PERFORMING ARTIST
JACKIE WILSON
ALBUM TITLE
REET THE BEST OF PETITE
ART DIRECTOR
CHRISTOPHER AUSTOPCHUK
RECORD COMPANY
© COLUMBIA RECORDS

PERFORMING ARTIST
MICK JAGGER
ALBUM TITLE
PRIMITIVE COOL
ART DIRECTOR
CHRISTOPHER AUSTOPCHUK

ILLUSTRATOR
FRANCESCO CLEMENTE
RECORD COMPANY
© COLUMBIA RECORDS

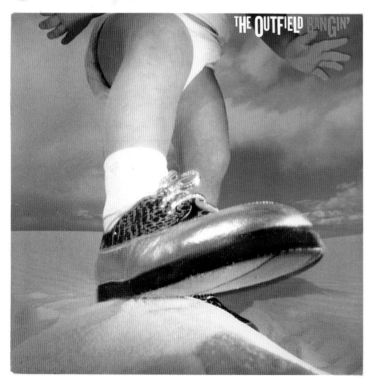

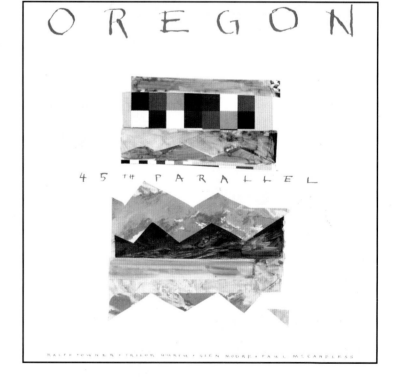

PERFORMING ARTIST
THE OUTFIELD
ALBUM TITLE
BANGIN'
ART DIRECTOR
CHRISTOPHER AUSTOPCHUK

RECORD COMPANY
© COLUMBIA RECORDS
PHOTOGRAPHER
CHIP SIMONS

PERFORMING ARTIST
OREGON
ALBUM TITLE
45TH PARALLEL
ART DIRECTOR
CHRISTOPHER AUSTOPCHUK

ILLUSTRATOR
BOB COTO
RECORD COMPANY
© EPIC/PORTRAIT

PERFORMING ARTIST
DUKE ELLINGTON
ALBUM TITLE
THE IMMORTAL 1938 YEAR BRAGGIN' IN BRASS
ART DIRECTOR
CHRISTOPHER AUSTOPCHUK
ILLUSTRATOR
GARY PANTER
RECORD COMPANY
© COLUMBIA RECORDS

STEPHEN AVERILL

BORN IN 1950 IN DUBLIN, IRELAND, STEPHEN AVERILL STARTED WORKING IN THE ADVERTISING INDUSTRY IN THE LATE '60S. HE COMBINED HIS STRONG INTEREST IN MUSIC AND DESIGN IN VARIOUS EXTRA-CURRICULAR ACTIVITIES WHICH CAME TO A HEAD WHEN HE CO-FOUNDED THE BAND "THE RADIATORS (FROM SPACE)" IN 1976, CONTRIBUTING TO THE BAND'S GRAPHIC OUTPUT AND MUSICAL STYLE. THE BAND MOVED TO LONDON, AND HE DECIDED TO REMAIN IN DUBLIN.

A LOCAL BAND PARTLY BASED IN HIS NEIGHBORHOOD APPROACHED HIM FOR ADVICE AND GRAPHIC WORK. HE CONTRIBUTED BOTH THE NAME AND THEIR FIRST POSTERS AND SLEEVES. THAT BAND, U2, WENT ON TO WORLDWIDE SUCCESS. THEY HAVE WORKED TOGETHER SINCE THAT TIME.

IT IS ONLY IN THE LAST FOUR YEARS THAT HE HAS SET UP HIS OWN COMPANY, WORKS ASSOCIATES.

PERFORMING ARTIST
U2
SINGLE TITLES
IN GOD'S COUNTRY
WHERE THE STREETS HAVE NO NAME
I STILL HAVEN'T FOUND WHAT I'M LOOKING FOR
WITH OR WITHOUT YOU
DESIGNER
STEPHEN AVERILL
RECORD COMPANY
© ISLAND RECORDS
PHOTOGRAPHER
ANTON CORBIJN

PERFORMING ARTIST
U2
ALBUM TITLE
THE JOSHUA TREE
DESIGNER
STEPHEN AVERILL
RECORD COMPANY
© ISLAND RECORDS
PHOTOGRAPHER
ANTON CORBIJN

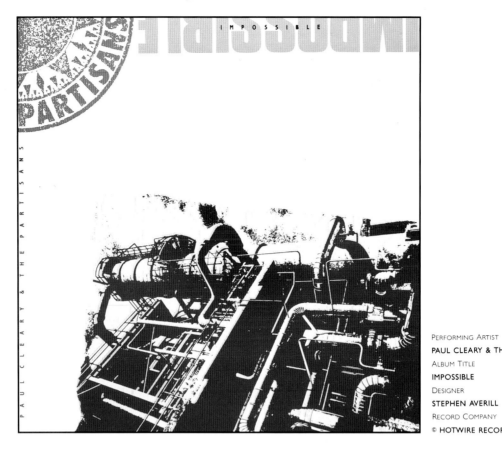

PERFORMING ARTIST
PAUL CLEARY & THE PARTISANS
ALBUM TITLE
IMPOSSIBLE
DESIGNER
STEPHEN AVERILL
RECORD COMPANY
© HOTWIRE RECORDS (IRELAND ONLY)

PERFORMING ARTIST
IN TUA NUA
SINGLE TITLE
BLUE EYES AGAIN
DESIGNER
STEPHEN AVERILL
RECORD COMPANY
© CBS RECORDS

PERFORMING ARTIST
SWIM
ALBUM TITLE
SUNDRIVE ROAD
DESIGNER
STEPHEN AVERILL
RECORD COMPANY
© **MCA RECORDS**
PHOTOGRAPHERS
ROBBIE JONES
8MM PHOTOGRAPHY —
CONOR HORGAN

PERFORMING ARTIST
AN EMOTIONAL FISH
ALBUM TITLE
AN EMOTIONAL FISH
DESIGNER
STEPHEN AVERILL
RECORD COMPANY
© **EAST-WEST RECORDS**
PHOTOGRAPHER
CONOR HORGAN

PERFORMING ARTIST
DOLORES KEANE
SINGLE TITLE
LION IN A CAGE
DESIGNER
STEPHEN AVERILL
RECORD COMPANY
© **ROUND TOWER RECORDS**
PHOTOGRAPHER
AMELIA STEIN

MICHAEL BAYS

MICHAEL BAYS IS RESPONSIBLE FOR ALBUM PACKAGING, ADVERTISING, AS WELL AS THE MERCHANDISING FOR THE POLYGRAM FAMILY OF ARTISTS.

UNDER HIS SUPERVISION, THE DEPARTMENT HAS RECEIVED NUMEROUS AWARDS AND HAS BEEN A PIONEER IN THE USE OF MACINTOSH COMPUTERS. HE HAS WON A GRAMMY AND CEBA AWARD AND IS A VOTING MEMBER OF THEIR PACKAGING COMMITTEES.

HE HAS BEEN A GUEST SPEAKER ON MTV AND ON MANY PANELS IN REFERENCE TO ALBUM PACKAGING. HE IS STILL EAGERLY AWAITING THE OPPORTUNITY TO DESIGN HIS OWN ALBUM PACKAGE AND BEGIN A WORLDWIDE TOUR.

PERFORMING ARTIST
JAMES BROWN
ALBUM TITLE
JAMES BROWN
DESIGNER
SHERYL LUTZ-BROWN
ART DIRECTOR
MICHAEL BAYS
ILLUSTRATOR
SCOTT TOWNSEND
RECORD COMPANY
POLYGRAM RECORDS

© 1991 POLYGRAM RECORDS, INC.

PERFORMING ARTIST
CHICKASAW MUDD PUPPIES
ALBUM TITLE
DO YOU REMEMBER (12" SINGLE)
DESIGNER
MICHAEL KLOTZ
ART DIRECTOR
MICHAEL BAYS
RECORD COMPANY
POLYGRAM RECORDS

© 1991 POLYGRAM RECORDS, INC.

PERFORMING ARTIST
VARIOUS ARTISTS
ALBUM TITLE
STAIRWAY TO HEAVEN/HIGHWAY TO HELL
DESIGNER
MARGERY GREENSPAN
ART DIRECTOR
MICHAEL BAYS
ILLUSTRATOR
BOB TILLERY (HUNGRY DOG STUDIO)
RECORD COMPANY
POLYGRAM RECORDS

© 1989 POLYGRAM RECORDS, INC.

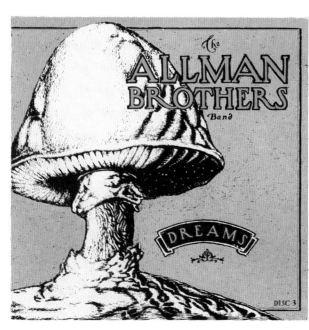

PERFORMING ARTIST
ALLMAN BROTHERS BAND
ALBUM TITLE
DREAMS CD PACKAGE
DESIGNER
MICHAEL KLOTZ
ART DIRECTOR
MICHAEL BAYS
RECORD COMPANY
POLYGRAM RECORDS

© 1989 POLYGRAM RECORDS, INC.

PERFORMING ARTIST
VARIOUS ARTISTS
ALBUM TITLE
IT'S A BEAUTIFUL THING
POLYGRAM'S SUMMER GROOVES (PROMOTIONAL CD)
DESIGNER
ALLI TRUCH
ART DIRECTOR
MICHAEL BAYS
RECORD COMPANY
POLYGRAM RECORDS

© 1990 POLYGRAM RECORDS, INC.

PERFORMING ARTIST
GEAR DADDIES
ALBUM TITLE
BILLY'S LIVE BAIT—PROMOTIONAL CD
DESIGNER
MITCHELL KANNER
ART DIRECTOR
MICHAEL BAYS
RECORD COMPANY
POLYGRAM RECORDS

© 1991 POLYGRAM RECORDS, INC.

JOHN BERG

A GRADUATE OF COOPER UNION, JOHN BERG JOINED COLUMBIA

RECORDS IN 1961 AS ART DIRECTOR OF PACKAGING. IN 1969, HE

BECAME CREATIVE DIRECTOR AND THEN BECAME VICE PRESIDENT

OF CBS RECORDS IN 1973. HE HAS BEEN RESPONSIBLE FOR THE

GRAPHICS FOR OVER 5,000 RECORDS SINCE THAT TIME. HE HAS

BEEN AN INSTRUCTOR AT PARSONS SCHOOL OF DESIGN.

HE HAS WON MANY AWARDS FOR HIS WORK INCLUDING FOUR

GRAMMYS (ACADEMY AWARDS) FOR BEST COVER OF THE YEAR FROM

NARAS AND THREE GOLD MEDALS FROM THE ART DIRECTORS CLUB

OF NEW YORK. HE HAS LECTURED AT VARIOUS INSTITUTIONS

INCLUDING TYLER INSTITUTE, SCHOOL OF VISUAL ARTS, COOPER

UNION AND THE NEW YORK, CINCINNATI, TORONTO AND

DALLAS/FORT WORTH ART DIRECTOR CLUBS.

PERFORMING ARTIST
FRANK SINATRA
ALBUM TITLE
RARITIES—THE COLUMBIA YEARS
DESIGNER
JOHN BERG
RECORD COMPANY
COLUMBIA RECORDS

© SONY MUSIC

PERFORMING ARTIST
FRANK SINATRA
ALBUM TITLE
**FRANK SINATRA—THE VOICE
THE COLUMBIA YEARS**
DESIGNER
JOHN BERG
ARTIST, HAND COLORING
KEN ROBBINS
RECORD COMPANY
COLUMBIA RECORDS

© SONY MUSIC

PERFORMING ARTIST
CHICAGO
ALBUM TITLE
CHICAGO VI
DESIGNER
JOHN BERG
ARTIST
NICK FASCIANO AND THE AMERICAN BANKNOTE COMPANY

© SONY MUSIC

PERFORMING ARTIST
CHICAGO
ALBUM TITLE
CHICAGO X
DESIGNER
JOHN BERG
ARTIST
NICK FASCIANO
RECORD COMPANY
COLUMBIA RECORDS
PHOTOGRAPHER
COLUMBIA RECORDS STUDIO

© SONY MUSIC

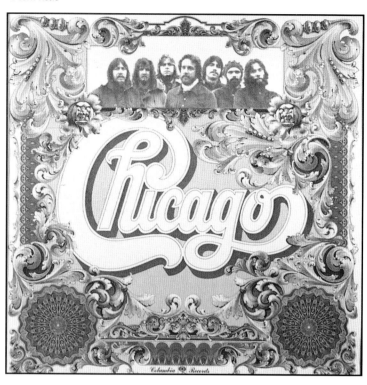

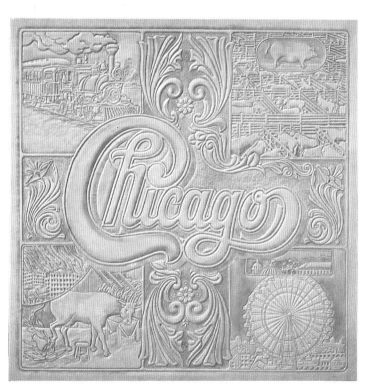

PERFORMING ARTIST   ARTIST
CHICAGO   **NICK FASCIANO**
ALBUM TITLE   RECORD COMPANY
CHICAGO VII   **COLUMBIA RECORDS**
DESIGNER
JOHN BERG   © SONY MUSIC

PERFORMING ARTIST   RECORD COMPANY
CHICAGO   **COLUMBIA RECORDS**
ALBUM TITLE   PHOTOGRAPHER
CHICAGO GREATEST HITS   **REID MILES**
DESIGNER
JOHN BERG   © SONY MUSIC

PERFORMING ARTIST
SANTANA
ALBUM TITLE
GREATEST HITS
DESIGNER
JOHN BERG
RECORD COMPANY
COLUMBIA RECORDS
PHOTOGRAPHER
JOEL BALDWIN

© SONY MUSIC

PERFORMING ARTIST
THE BYRDS
ALBUM TITLE
BYRDMANIAX
DESIGNERS
JOHN BERG AND VIRGINIA TEAM
ARTIST
LIFE MASKS
RECORD COMPANY
COLUMBIA RECORDS

© SONY MUSIC

CAROL BOBOLTS

CAROL BOBOLTS IS A FOUNDER AND PRINCIPAL OF RED HERRING DESIGN, A NEW YORK BASED GRAPHICS AND ART DIRECTION FIRM. HER CLIENTS INCLUDE ATLANTIC RECORDS, ELEKTRA RECORDS, CAPITOL RECORDS, WARNER BROS. RECORDS, CHARISMA RECORDS, SBK RECORDS, ATCO RECORDS, ASSOCIATED VIRGIN LABELS, ISLAND RECORDS AND VARIOUS OTHERS OUTSIDE OF THE ENTERTAINMENT INDUSTRY.

PRIOR TO FOUNDING RED HERRING, CAROL WAS EMPLOYED BY ATLANTIC RECORDS AND WAS RESPONSIBLE FOR ELEKTRA RECORDS PACKAGING, MERCHANDISING AND ADVERTISING. SHE WAS ALSO WITH THE RENOWNED DESIGN FIRM PUSHPIN LUBALIN PECKOLICK AND THE DESIGN CENTER OF THE COOPER UNION FOR THE ADVANCEMENT OF SCIENCE AND ART.

HER WORK HAS RECEIVED AWARDS FROM THE ART DIRECTORS CLUB OF LOS ANGELES, THE TYPE DIRECTOR'S CLUB, AND AIGA AND HAS BEEN PUBLISHED IN PRINT AND COMMUNICATION ARTS. IN 1990, SHE WAS NOMINATED FOR A GRAMMY AWARD FOR BEST PACKAGE DESIGN.

MS. BOBOLTS BEGAN HER DESIGN STUDIES AT THE UNIVERSITY OF MICHIGAN AND GRADUATED FROM THE COOPER UNION.

PERFORMING ARTIST
PHOEBE SNOW
ALBUM TITLE
SOMETHING REAL
DESIGNER AND ART DIRECTOR
CAROL BOBOLTS
RECORD COMPANY
ELEKTRA RECORDS
PHOTÖGRAPHER
MICHELLE CLEMENT

© 1989 ELEKTRA RECORDS

PERFORMING ARTIST
TRACY CHAPMAN
ALBUM TITLE
TRACY CHAPMAN
DESIGNER AND ART DIRECTOR
CAROL BOBOLTS
RECORD COMPANY
ELEKTRA RECORDS
PHOTOGRAPHER
MATT MAHURIN

© 1988 ELEKTRA RECORDS

KEITH BREEDEN

IN 1986, KEITH BREEDEN SET UP DKB. CURRENTLY, DKB CONSISTS OF
3 PEOPLE—KEITH BREEDEN, PETER CURZON AND MARTIN JENKINS.
DKB MAINLY WORKS IN MUSIC DESIGN CREATING LOGOS,
PACKAGING, POSTERS, ADVERTISING AND T-SHIRTS. THEY WORK
WITH A VARIETY OF CLIENTS AND PREFER TO WORK WITH
MUSICIANS WHOSE WORK THEY RESPECT AS IT SERVES AS AN
INSPIRATION. WITH THE EXCEPTION OF PHOTOGRAPHY, ALMOST
ALL THE ELEMENTS WITHIN DESIGN—PAINTINGS, GRAPHICS,
CALLIGRAPHY AND SCULPTURE—IS PRODUCED IN HOUSE BY ONE
OF THE 3 DESIGNERS. THEY WORK IN A STYLE THAT IS APPROPRIATE
TO THE CLIENT AND PROJECT.

THEY HAVE WORKED WITH ABC, THE CULT, BRYAN FERRY, FINE
YOUNG CANNIBALS, THE MISSION, ALISON MOYET AND SCRITTI
POLITTI.

PERFORMING ARTIST
FINE YOUNG CANNIBALS
ALBUM TITLE
I'M NOT THE MAN I USED TO BE
DESIGNERS
KEITH BREEDEN AND MARTIN JENKINS, DKB
RECORD COMPANY
LONDON RECORDS

© KEITH BREEDEN AND MARTIN JENKINS, DKB

PERFORMING ARTIST
FINE YOUNG CANNIBALS
ALBUM TITLE
SHE DRIVES ME CRAZY
DESIGNER
MARTIN JENKINS, DKB
RECORD COMPANY
LONDON RECORDS

© MARTIN JENKINS, DKB

PERFORMING ARTIST
FINE YOUNG CANNIBALS
ALBUM TITLE
GOOD THING
DESIGNERS
KEITH BREEDEN AND MARTIN JENKINS
RECORD COMPANY
LONDON RECORDS

© KEITH BREEDEN AND MARTIN JENKINS, DKB

PERFORMING ARTIST
SCRITTI POLITTI
ALBUM TITLE
OH PATTI
DESIGNERS
KEITH BREEDEN, GARTSIDE, DKB
RECORD COMPANY
VIRGIN RECORDS

© KEITH BREEDEN, GARTSIDE, DKB

PERFORMING ARTIST
COLOURS
ALBUM TITLE
SOMEONE TO LOVE
DESIGNER
PETER CURZON, DKB
RECORD COMPANY
EAST WEST RECORDS

© PETER CURZON, DKB

PERFORMING ARTIST
THE CULT
ALBUM TITLE
ELECTRIC
DESIGNERS
KEITH BREEDEN AND STORM THORGERSON
RECORD COMPANY
BEGGARS BANQUET

© KEITH BREEDEN AND STORM THORGERSON

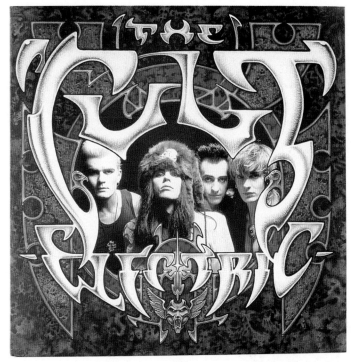

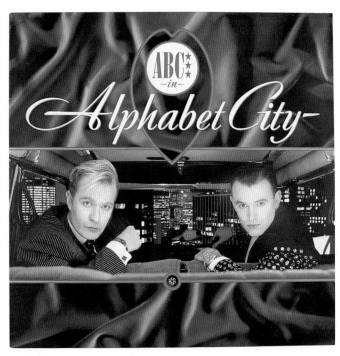

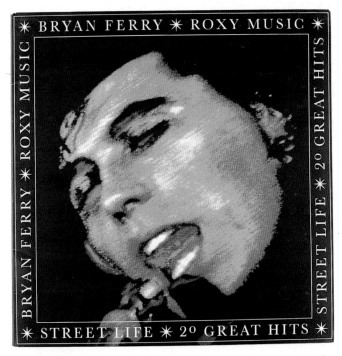

PERFORMING ARTIST
ABC
ALBUM TITLE
ALPHABET CITY
DESIGNERS
KEITH BREEDEN AND PETER CURZON, DKB
RECORD COMPANY
NEUTRON RECORDS

© KEITH BREEDEN AND PETER CURZON, DKB

PERFORMING ARTIST
BRYAN FERRY & ROXY MUSIC
ALBUM TITLE
STREET LIFE
DESIGNERS
KEITH BREEDEN, DKB
RECORD COMPANY
EG RECORDS

© KEITH BREEDEN, DKB

STEVE BYRAM

BORN IN 1952 IN OAKLAND, CALIFORNIA, STEPHEN BYRAM STUDIED ART AT THE ACADEMY OF ART, SAN FRANCISCO. AFTER MOVING TO NEW YORK IN 1979, HE WORKED FOR STIFF AMERICA, RCA RECORDS AND THEN BECAME AN ART DIRECTOR FOR CBS (NOW SONY) RECORDS. HE LEFT CBS IN 1990 AND HAS CONTINUED DESIGNING FOR ELEKTRA, JMT RECORDS, NEW WORLD/COUNTERCURRENTS AND MTV. HE IS ALSO AN INSTRUCTOR AT THE SCHOOL OF VISUAL ARTS AND LIVES IN NEW JERSEY WITH HIS WIFE AND DOG AND WORKS IN THE BASEMENT, QUITE HAPPILY.

PERFORMING ARTIST

SLAMMIN' WATUSIS

ALBUM TITLE

KINGS OF NOISE

DESIGNER, ART DIRECTOR AND COVER PAINTER

STEPHEN BYRAM

RECORD COMPANY

EPIC RECORDS

PHOTOGRAPHER

TONY SOLURI

© 1989 EPIC RECORDS

PERFORMING ARTIST

MIDNIGHT OIL

ALBUM TITLE

THE GREEN DISC

DESIGNER AND ART DIRECTOR

STEPHEN BYRAM

ILLUSTRATOR

STEPHEN KRONINGER

COPYWRITER

BECKY NEIMAN

RECORD COMPANY

CBS RECORDS

© 1990 CBS RECORDS

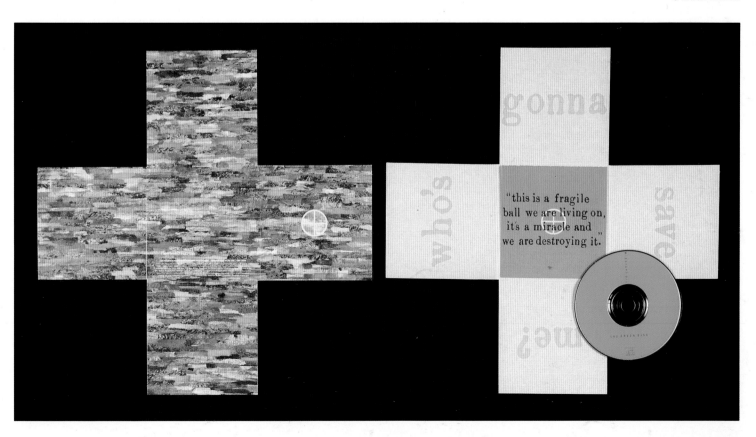

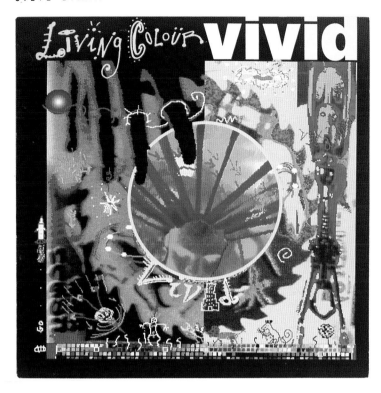

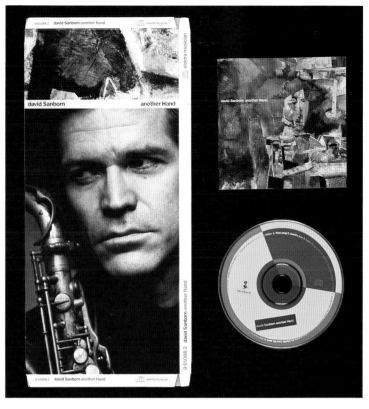

PERFORMING ARTIST
LIVING COLOUR
ALBUM TITLE
VIVID
DESIGNER
THE THUNDERJOCKEYS
ART DIRECTOR
STEPHEN BYRAM
RECORD COMPANY
EPIC RECORDS

© 1988 EPIC RECORDS

PERFORMING ARTIST
DAVID SANBORN
ALBUM TITLE
ANOTHER HAND
(LONG BOX, CD BOOKLET AND DISC)
DESIGNER, ART DIRECTOR AND PAINTER
STEPHEN BYRAM
RECORD COMPANY
ELEKTRA RECORDS
PHOTOGRAPHER
ROY VOLKMANN

© 1991 ELEKTRA RECORDS

PERFORMING ARTIST
TIM BERNE
ALBUM TITLE
SANCTIFIED DREAMS
DESIGNER, ART DIRECTOR AND COVER PAINTER
STEPHEN BYRAM
RECORD COMPANY
COLUMBIA RECORDS
PHOTOGRAPHER
MARK MALABRIGO

© 1987 COLUMBIA RECORDS

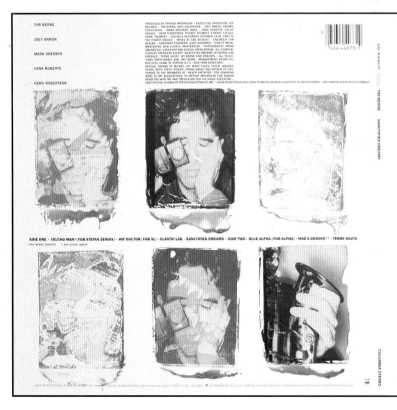

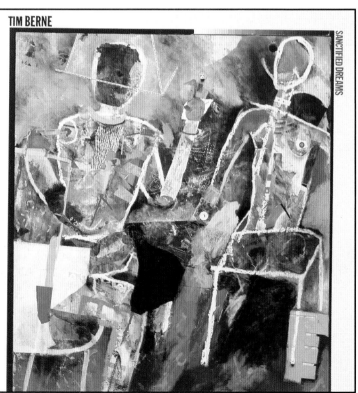

PERFORMING ARTIST
MATTHEW SWEET
ALBUM TITLE
INSIDE
DESIGNER AND ART DIRECTOR
STEPHEN BYRAM
RECORD COMPANY
COLUMBIA RECORDS
PHOTOGRAPHER
HARRIS SAVIDES

© 1986 COLUMBIA RECORDS

PERFORMING ARTIST
THE BEASTIE BOYS
ALBUM TITLE
LICENSED TO ILL
ART DIRECTOR
STEPHEN BYRAM
COVER ART
DAVID GAMBALE
RECORD COMPANY
COLUMBIA/DEF JAM RECORDS

© 1986 COLUMBIA/DEF JAM RECORDS

KIM CHAMPAGNE

KIM CHAMPAGNE WAS BORN AND RAISED IN CANADA. AFTER
GRADUATING FROM THE ALBERTA COLLEGE OF ART IN 1984, SHE
HEADED SOUTH TO LOS ANGELES. SHE IS CURRENTLY CONSULTANT
SR. ART DIRECTOR AT WARNER BROS. RECORDS WHERE SHE HAS
WORKED FOR THE PAST FIVE YEARS. HER WORK HAS APPEARED
IN VARIOUS PUBLICATIONS INCLUDING PRINT AND CA. SHE HAS
RECEIVED AWARDS FROM THE AIGA, THE NEW YORK ART DIRECTORS
CLUB AND OTHERS. SHE WAS NOMINATED FOR A GRAMMY IN THE
CATEGORY OF BEST ALBUM PACKAGE IN 1991.

PERFORMING ARTIST
BODEANS
ALBUM TITLE
BLACK & WHITE
DESIGNER AND ART DIRECTOR
KIM CHAMPAGNE
RECORD COMPANY
SLASH RECORDS
PHOTOGRAPHER
STUART WATSON
BAND PHOTOGRAPHER
MICHAEL WILSON

© 1991 SLASH RECORDS

PERFORMING ARTIST
BODEANS
ALBUM TITLE
BLACK & WHITE (PROMOTIONAL FOLDING POSTCARDS)
DESIGNER
KIM CHAMPAGNE
ART DIRECTORS
KIM CHAMPAGNE AND LIZ SILVERMAN
RECORD COMPANY
SLASH RECORDS
PHOTOGRAPHER
MICHAEL WILSON

© 1991 SLASH RECORDS

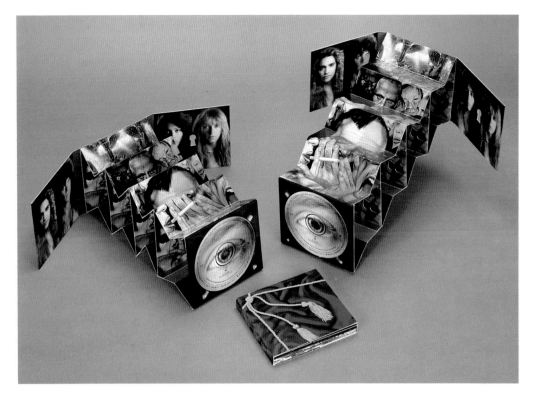

PERFORMING ARTIST
THE BULLET BOYS
ALBUM TITLE
FREAKSHOW (DIGISCOPE)
DESIGNER
KIM CHAMPAGNE
ART DIRECTORS
KIM CHAMPAGNE AND JE
ILLUSTRATOR
DAVID B. MCMACKEN

DIGISCOPE CONCEPTION
JIM LADWIG
RECORD COMPANY
WARNER BROTHERS RECORDS
BAND PHOTOGRAPHER
AARON RAPOPORT
VELVET PHOTOGRAPHER
VICTOR BRACKE

© 1991 WARNER BROTHERS RECORDS, INC.

PERFORMING ARTIST
TERRELL
ALBUM TITLE
**ON THE WINGS OF DIRTY ANGELS
(PROMOTIONAL DIGIPAK)**
DESIGNER AND ART DIRECTOR
KIM CHAMPAGNE
RECORD COMPANY
GIANT RECORDS
PHOTOGRAPHER
MARK ABRAHAMS

© 1990 GIANT RECORDS

PERFORMING ARTIST
THE REPLACEMENTS
ALBUM TITLE
ALL SHOOK DOWN
DESIGNER
REY INTERNATIONAL MR/GL
ART DIRECTOR
KIM CHAMPAGNE AND MICHAEL REY
RECORD COMPANY
SIRE RECORDS
PHOTOGRAPHER
MICHAEL WILSON

© 1990 SIRE RECORDS COMPANY

PERFORMING ARTIST
LONE JUSTICE
ALBUM TITLE
SHELTER
DESIGNER
KIM CHAMPAGNE
COVER IMAGE
COOPER EDENS
RECORD COMPANY
GEFFEN RECORDS
BAND PHOTOGRAPHER
MELANIE NISSEN

© 1986 THE DAVID GEFFEN COMPANY

PERFORMING ARTIST
LONE JUSTICE
ALBUM TITLE
SHELTER (MAXI-SINGLE)
DESIGNER AND ART DIRECTOR
KIM CHAMPAGNE
RECORD COMPANY
GEFFEN RECORDS

© 1986 THE DAVID GEFFEN COMPANY

43

PETER CORRISTON

PETER CORRISTON STUDIED PAINTING AND PHOTOGRAPHY (1967–1972) IN NEW YORK, ROME AND SAN FRANCISCO. HIS FIRST CLIENTS INCLUDED CHEECH AND CHONG, NEW YORK DOLLS, AND ROD STEWART. HE WAS NOMINATED FOR FOUR GRAMMY AWARDS FOR "BEST PACKAGING" CATEGORY IN 1972, 1974, 1975 AND 1980 AND IN 1982, WON THIS GRAMMY FOR THE ROLLING STONES "TATTOO YOU." "HIS WORLD PARTY" 1991 DESIGN WAS SELECTED INTO THE PERMANENT COLLECTION OF THE LIBRARY OF CONGRESS.

IN 1990, HE DEVELOPED THE CORPORATE ID FOR MCA LABEL "INFINITY." SOME OF HIS MOST RECENT CLIENTS INCLUDE TOM WAITS, MICK JAGGER, PAT BENATAR, SINEAD O'CONNER, THE ROLLING STONES, AND BILLY IDOL. HE IS CURRENTLY WORKING IN NEW YORK CITY.

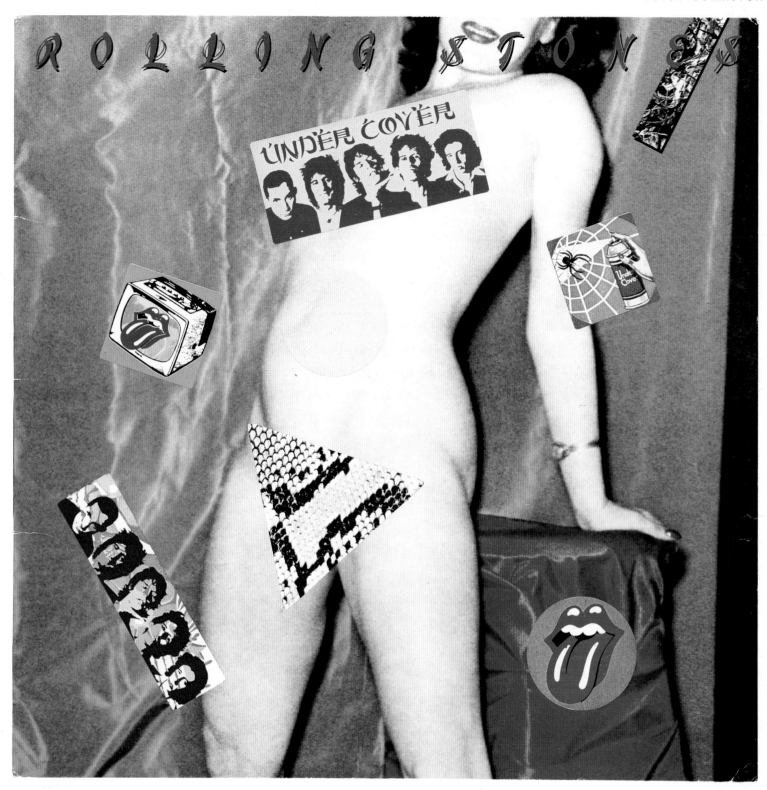

PERFORMING ARTIST
THE ROLLING STONES
ALBUM TITLE
UNDER COVER
DESIGNER
PETER CORRISTON
RECORD COMPANY
ATLANTIC RECORDS
PHOTOGRAPHER
HUBERT KRETZSCHMAN

© 1984 ATLANTIC RECORDS

PERFORMING ARTIST
ROD STEWART
ALBUM TITLE
SING IT AGAIN ROD
DESIGNER
PETER CORRISTON
RECORD COMPANY
PHONOGRAM/MERCURY RECORDS
PHOTOGRAPHER
COMSO

© 1973 PHONOGRAM/MERCURY RECORDS

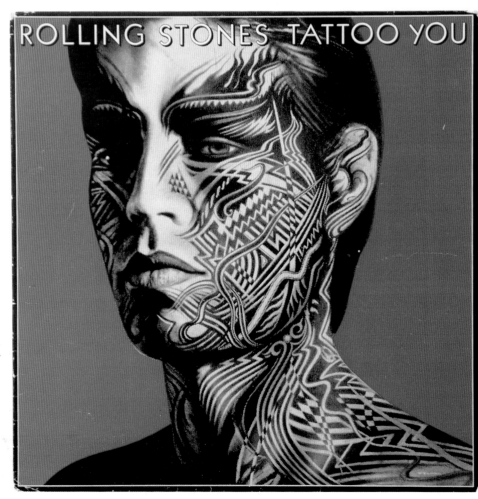

PERFORMING ARTIST
THE ROLLING STONES
ALBUM TITLE
TATTOO YOU
DESIGNER AND ART DIRECTOR
PETER CORRISTON
ILLUSTRATOR
CHRISTIAN PIPER
RECORD COMPANY
ROLLING STONES RECORDS

© 1982 ROLLING STONES RECORDS

PERFORMING ARTIST
WORLD PARTY
ALBUM TITLE
GOODBYE JUMBO
DESIGNER
PETER CORRISTON
RECORD COMPANY
ENSIGN/CHRYSALIS RECORDS
PHOTOGRAPHER
HUBERT KRETZSCHMAN

© 1990 ENSIGN RECORDS

PERFORMING ARTIST
THE ANGELS
ALBUM TITLE
DOGS ARE TALKING
DESIGNERS AND ART DIRECTORS
PETER CORRISTON AND PAT MCGOWAN
RECORD COMPANY
CHRYSALIS RECORDS
PHOTOGRAPHERS
PETER CORRISTON AND PAT MCGOWAN

© 1989 CHRYSALIS RECORDS, INC.

MARC COZZA

MARC COZZA GRADUATED FROM THE TYLER SCHOOL OF ART IN 1984 WHERE HE STUDIED UNDER THE POLISH ILLUSTRATOR STANISLAW ZAGORSKI AND THE ART DIRECTOR PETER CORRISTON. THEY WERE BOTH BIG INFLUENCES ON HIM. AFTER GRADUATION, HE LEFT PHILADELPHIA FOR NEW YORK WITH A HANDFUL OF REFERRALS. HE WAS HIRED AS A DESIGNER BY ROGER GORMAN TO WORK IN HIS NEW STUDIO, REINER DESIGN. AT THE SAME TIME, HE CREATED BOOKCOVER ILLUSTRATIONS FOR ST. MARTIN'S PRESS AND SOME ALBUM COVER ARTWORK. HE LEFT REINER AFTER A YEAR, AND CONTINUED WITH HIS ILLUSTRATION WORK BUT WISHED FOR MORE VARIETY IN HIS ASSIGNMENTS. AFTER A LENGTHY TRIP TO EUROPE, HE WORKED FOR A SHORT TIME DESIGNING A SPECIAL ISSUE OF TRAVEL & LEISURE MAGAZINE.

IN 1987, COZZA WAS HIRED AS A DESIGNER TO HELP START THE IN-HOUSE ART DEPARTMENT AT CHRYSALIS RECORDS ALONG WITH HIS FORMER TEACHER, CORRISTON. FOR 3 YEARS THEY CREATED A VARIETY OF PACKAGING AND ADVERTISING GRAPHICS TOGETHER. IN 1990, COZZA WAS PROMOTED TO SENIOR ART DIRECTOR OVERSEEING THE ART DEPARTMENT AT CHRYSALIS.

PERFORMING ARTIST
WORLD PARTY
SINGLE TITLE
WAY DOWN NOW
DESIGNER
MARC COZZA
RECORD COMPANY
ENSIGN/CHRYSALIS RECORDS
COVER ART
HUBERT KRETZSCHMAR

© 1990 ENSIGN RECORDS, LTD./CHRYSALIS RECORDS, INC.

PERFORMING ARTIST
BOBCAT GOLDTHWAIT
ALBUM TITLE
MEAT BOB
DESIGNERS AND ART DIRECTORS
PETER CORRISTON AND MARC COZZA
RECORD COMPANY
CHRYSALIS RECORDS
PHOTOGRAPHERS
JAMIE AMRINE AND BRIAN HAGIWARA

© 1988 CHRYSALIS RECORDS, INC.

PERFORMING ARTIST
G LOVE E
ALBUM TITLE
DANCE BABY
DESIGNER AND ART DIRECTOR
MARC COZZA

ILLUSTRATOR
CALEF BROWN
RECORD COMPANY
CHRYSALIS RECORDS

© 1990 CHRYSALIS RECORDS, INC.

PERFORMING ARTIST
BROKEN GLASS
ALBUM TITLE
A FAST MEAN GAME
DESIGNER AND ART DIRECTOR
MARC COZZA

RECORD COMPANY
CHRYSALIS RECORDS
PHOTOGRAPHER
BRIAN HAGIWARA

© 1990 CHRYSALIS RECORDS, INC.

ROGER DEAN

ROGER DEAN WAS BORN IN KENT, ENGLAND, IN 1944. HE STUDIED INDUSTRIAL DESIGN AT CANTERBURY COLLEGE OF ART, AND IN 1968 WENT ON TO THE ROYAL COLLEGE OF ART. HIS RECORD COVERS AND ASSOCIATED GRAPHICS—LOGOS AND LETTERING, CREATED A NEW GENRE OF WORK. DURING THE '60S HE ESTABLISHED HIMSELF AS A SUCCESSFUL ARTIST WITH AN INTERNATIONAL REPUTATION. HIS POSTERS, PRINTS AND BOOKS HAVE SOLD IN MILLIONS WORLDWIDE. SINCE 1975, HE HAS HELD SEVERAL SOLO EXHIBITIONS, INCLUDING THOSE AT THE INSTITUTE OF COMTEMPORARY ART, AND AT THE NEW YORK CULTURAL CENTER. AT THE TIME OF GOING TO PRESS HIS WORK IS ON SHOW AT THE SAN FRANCISCO ART EXCHANGE. HE HAS ALSO SET UP AND SUCCESSFULLY RUNS HIS OWN PUBLISHING COMPANY AND PIONEERED A UNIQUE FORM OF ARCHITECTURE. HE IS CURRENTLY INVOLVED IN THE DESIGN AND EXECUTION OF SEVERAL LARGE-SCALE ARCHITECTURAL PROJECTS.

PERFORMING ARTIST
YES
ALBUM TITLE
UNION
DESIGNER AND PAINTER
ROGER DEAN
RECORD COMPANY
ARISTA RECORDS

© 1991 ROGER DEAN

PERFORMING ARTIST
YES
ALBUM TITLE
YES YEARS
DESIGNER
ROGER DEAN
RECORD COMPANY
ATCO

© 1991 ROGER DEAN

PERFORMING ARTIST
ASIA
ALBUM TITLE
ALPHA
DESIGNER AND PAINTER
ROGER DEAN
RECORD COMPANY
GEFFEN RECORDS

© 1983 ROGER DEAN

PERFORMING ARTIST
DAVE GREENSLADE
ALBUM TITLE
CACTUS CHOIR
DESIGNER AND PAINTER
ROGER DEAN
RECORD COMPANY
WARNER BROTHERS RECORDS

© 1975 ROGER DEAN

PERFORMING ARTIST
YES
ALBUM TITLE
RELAYER
DESIGNER AND PAINTER
ROGER DEAN
RECORD COMPANY
ATLANTIC RECORDS

© 1974 ROGER DEAN

PERFORMING ARTIST
OSIBISA
ALBUM TITLE
WOYAYA
DESIGNER AND PAINTER
ROGER DEAN
RECORD COMPANY
MCA RECORDS

© 1972 ROGER DEAN

PERFORMING ARTIST
NIGHT WING
ALBUM TITLE
MY KINGDOM COME
DESIGNER AND PAINTER
ROGER DEAN

© 1984 ROGER DEAN

BOB DEFRIN

BORN IN NEW YORK CITY, BOB DEFRIN, FORMER VICE-PRESIDENT AND CREATIVE DIRECTOR OF GRAPHICS FOR ATLANTIC RECORDS AND CURRENTLY HEAD OF HIS OWN DESIGN FIRM, IS THE RECIPIENT OF NUMEROUS AWARDS FROM THE ART DIRECTORS CLUB (LOS ANGELES AND NEW YORK), INCLUDING THE GOLD MEDAL FROM THE NEW YORK CHAPTER, THE TYPE DIRECTORS CLUB, THE SOCIETY OF ILLUSTRATORS, AND THE AIGA.

DEFRIN ALSO HAS FOUR GRAMMY NOMINATIONS FOR RECORD ALBUM PACKAGING AND TWO POSTERS IN THE PERMANENT COLLECTION OF THE MUSEUM OF MODERN ART IN NEW YORK.

HE IS A MEMBER OF THE NATIONAL ACADEMY OF RECORDING ARTS & SCIENCES, THE ART DIRECTORS CLUB OF NEW YORK, THE TYPE DIRECTORS CLUB, AND THE AIGA.

PERFORMING ARTIST
LARRY CORYELL AND ALPHONSE MOUZON
ALBUM TITLE
BACK TOGETHER AGAIN
DESIGNER AND ART DIRECTOR
BOB DEFRIN

ILLUSTRATOR
ROGER HUYSSEN
RECORD COMPANY
ATLANTIC RECORDS

© ATLANTIC RECORDING CORP.

PERFORMING ARTIST
BILLY COBHAM
ALBUM TITLE
LIFE & TIMES
DESIGNER AND ART DIRECTOR
BOB DEFRIN

RECORD COMPANY
ATLANTIC RECORDS
PHOTOGRAPHER
FRANK MOSCATI

© ATLANTIC RECORDING CORP.

PERFORMING ARTIST
DAN SEALS
ALBUM TITLE
HARBINGER
DESIGNER AND ART DIRECTOR
BOB DEFRIN

RECORD COMPANY
ATLANTIC RECORDS
PHOTOGRAPHER
JIM MCGUIRE

© ATLANTIC RECORDING CORP.

PERFORMING ARTIST
EDDIE HARRIS
ALBUM TITLE
IS IT IN
DESIGNER AND ART DIRECTOR
BOB DEFRIN

ILLUSTRATOR
PETER PALOMISI
RECORD COMPANY
ATLANTIC RECORDS

© ATLANTIC RECORDING CORP.

SPENCER DRATE
JÜTKA SALAVETZ

SPENCER DRATE, AN ART DIRECTOR, DESIGNER AND CD
CONSULTANT, HAS DESIGNED MUSIC GRAPHICS FOR MANY NOTABLE
RECORDING ARTISTS INCLUDING LOU REED, TALKING HEADS, JOAN
JETT & THE BLACKHEARTS AND BON JOVI. HE WAS NOMINATED FOR
AN LP PACKAGING GRAMMY IN 1979, AND HIS WORK HAS BEEN
INCLUDED IN MANY NOTABLE DESIGN SHOWS. HE WAS THE FIRST
TO PIONEER THE IMPORTANCE OF THE GRAPHIC POSSIBILITES OF CD
SPECIAL PACKAGING. HIS EXPERTISE ON THIS SUBJECT HAS
RESULTED IN BEING INTERVIEWED BY THE NEW YORK TIMES, MTV,
VH-1, WOR-TV, PRINT MAGAZINE, BILLBOARD MAGAZINE AND MANY
OTHER PUBLICATIONS. MR. DRATE IS A MEMBER OF THE NATIONAL
ACADEMY OF RECORDING ARTS AND SCIENCES (NARAS) AND WAS
AN ALTERNATE MEMBER OF THE 1991 AND 1992 GRAMMY PACKAGING
COMMITTEE.

JÜTKA SALAVETZ, AN ART DIRECTOR AND DESIGNER, HAS DESIGNED
WITH SPENCER DRATE FOR THE PAST EIGHT YEARS. SHE HAS
WORKED FREELANCE FOR THE MOST PART AND CONTRIBUTED TO
MOST OF THE MUSIC DESIGNS BY JUSTDESIGN. JÜTKA HAS A B.A. IN
FINE ARTS WITH EMPHASIS ON GRAPHIC DESIGN. SHE TOO IS A
MEMBER OF NARAS.

PERFORMING ARTIST
JOAN JETT & THE BLACKHEARTS
ALBUM TITLE
ALBUM
DESIGNERS
SPENCER DRATE AND J. SALAVETZ
ART DIRECTORS
SPENCER DRATE, MERYL LAGUNA AND J. SALAVETZ
RECORD COMPANY
BLACKHEART RECORDS/MCA RECORDS
PHOTOGRAPHER
DIETER ZILL

© 1983 BLACKHEART RECORDS/MCA RECORDS

PERFORMING ARTIST
LOU REED
CD TITLE
METAL MEMORIAL EDITION CD
DESIGNER AND ART DIRECTOR
SYLVIA REED AND SPENCER DRATE
ADDITIONAL DESIGN: DENNIS ASCIENZO
RECORD COMPANY
SIRE/WARNER BROS.
COVER PHOTO
LOUIS JAMMES

© 1992 SIRE/WARNER BROS.

CD BOOKLET (INSIDE BOX)
DESIGNER AND ART DIRECTOR
SYLVIA REED AND SPENCER DRATE
ADDITIONAL DESIGN: J. SALAVETZ
AND DENNIS ASCIENZO
RECORD COMPANY
SIRE/WARNER BROS.
COVER PHOTO
LOUIS JAMMES

© 1992 SIRE/WARNER BROS.

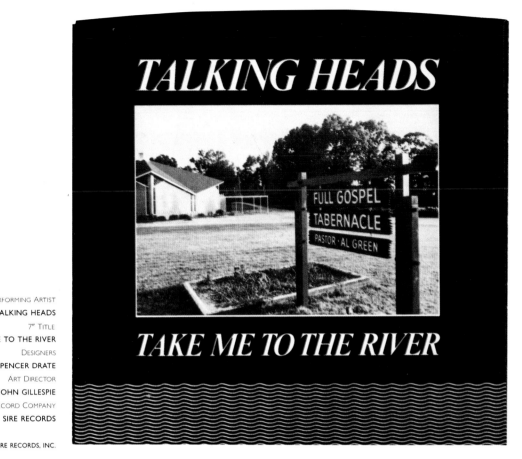

PERFORMING ARTIST
TALKING HEADS
7" TITLE
TAKE ME TO THE RIVER
DESIGNERS
DAVID BYRNE AND SPENCER DRATE
ART DIRECTOR
JOHN GILLESPIE
RECORD COMPANY
SIRE RECORDS

© 1978 SIRE RECORDS, INC.

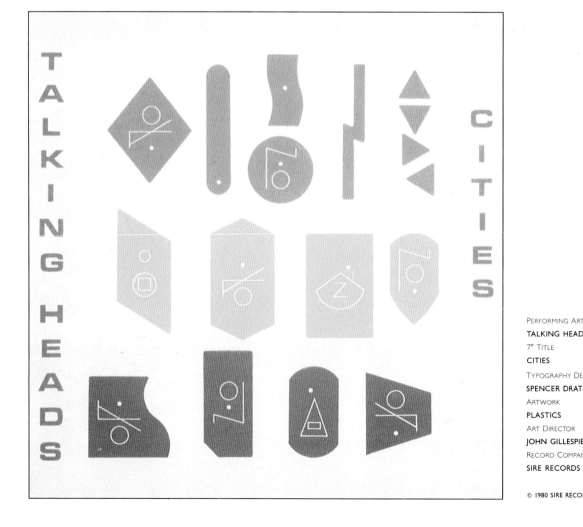

PERFORMING ARTIST
TALKING HEADS
7" TITLE
CITIES
TYPOGRAPHY DESIGN
SPENCER DRATE
ARTWORK
PLASTICS
ART DIRECTOR
JOHN GILLESPIE
RECORD COMPANY
SIRE RECORDS

© 1980 SIRE RECORDS, INC.

PERFORMING ARTIST
ROBERT ELLIS ORRALL

ALBUM TITLE
FIXATION

DESIGNER
SPENCER DRATE

ART DIRECTOR
ANOTHER RECORD CO.

ART
STEVE BYRAM AND DAVID GAMBALE

RECORD COMPANY
WHY-FI RECORDS, LTD.

© 1981 WHY-FI RECORDS, LTD.

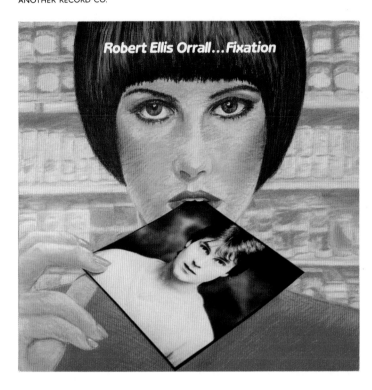

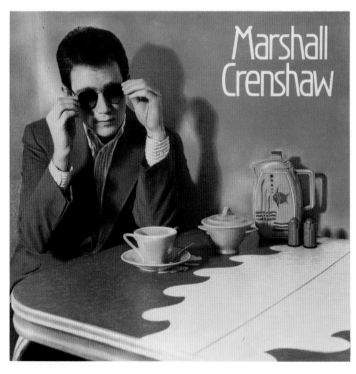

PERFORMING ARTIST
MARSHALL CRENSHAW

ALBUM TITLE
MARSHALL CRENSHAW

DESIGNER AND ART DIRECTOR
SPENCER DRATE

PHOTO OIL PAINTER
CHRISTINA DE LANCIE

RECORD COMPANY
WARNER BROTHERS RECORDS

PHOTOGRAPHER
GARY GREEN

© 1982 WARNER BROTHERS RECORDS, INC.

PERFORMING ARTIST
THE FABULOUS THUNDERBIRDS
ALBUM TITLE
TUFF ENUFF
DESIGNERS AND ART DIRECTORS
SPENCER DRATE AND J. SALAVETZ
ARTWORK
DAN YOUNGBLOOD
RECORD COMPANY
CBS RECORDS

© 1986 CBS RECORDS, INC.

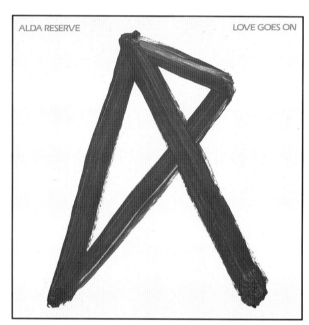

PERFORMING ARTIST
ALDA RESERVE
ALBUM TITLE
LOVE GOES ON
DESIGNERS
SPENCER DRATE AND BRAD ELLIS
ARTWORK
BRAD ELLIS
ART DIRECTOR
JOHN GILLESPIE
RECORD COMPANY
SIRE RECORDS
PHOTOGRAPHER
DEAN CHAMBERLAIN

© 1979 SIRE RECORDS COMPANY

PERFORMING ARTIST
VISIONS
ALBUM TITLE
HYPNOTIZED
DESIGNERS
SPENCER DRATE AND J. SALAVETZ
ART DIRECTOR
MICHAEL BAYS
RECORD COMPANY
POLYGRAM RECORDS

© 1988 POLYGRAM RECORDS, INC.

PERFORMING ARTIST
LOU REED
ALBUM AND CD TITLE
MAGIC AND LOSS
DESIGNERS
SYLVIA REED, SPENCER DRATE AND J. SALAVETZ
ART DIRECTORS
SYLVIA REED AND SPENCER DRATE
RECORD COMPANY
SIRE/WARNER BROTHERS RECORDS

© 1992 SIRE/WARNER BROTHERS RECORDS, INC.

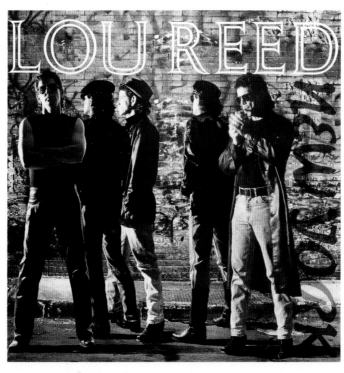

PERFORMING ARTIST
LOU REED
ALBUM AND CD TITLE
NEW YORK
DESIGNERS
SYLVIA REED AND SPENCER DRATE
ART DIRECTOR
SPENCER DRATE
PHOTOGRAPHER
WARING ABBOTT

© 1989 SIRE RECORDS COMPANY

ROD DYER

AWARD-WINNING ART DIRECTOR/DESIGNER ROD DYER BEGAN HIS CAREER IN GRAPHIC ARTS AT KENYON ADVERTISING IN HIS NATIVE SOUTH AFRICA. HE EMIGRATED TO THE UNITED STATES AND WORKED AT GORE/SMITH/GREENLAND IN NEW YORK AND WORKED HIS WAY TO LOS ANGELES IN 1960.

HE WORKED AT JEROME GOULD & ASSOCIATES, CARSON/ROBERTS ADVERTISING, THE OFFICE OF CHARLES EAMES, AND CAPITOL RECORDS WHICH HE LEFT IN 1967 TO FORM HIS OWN DESIGN FIRM, ROD DYER, INC., AND SOON AFTER WAS DOING AWARD-WINNING WORK FOR ALMOST EVERY RECORD LABEL IN THE COUNTRY. HIS CLIENT LIST ENCOMPASSES MANY INDUSTRIES INCLUDING FASHION, ENTERTAINMENT, AEROSPACE AND MANY MORE. ROD BEGAN TO DIRECT AND OVERSEE VARIOUS VIDEO — TRAILERS AND INDUSTRIAL FILMS.

HE HAS WON VARIOUS AWARDS INCLUDING THE ART DIRECTORS CLUB OF NEW YORK AND LOS ANGELES, THE BELDING AWARD, AND THE HAMANO INSTITUTE, TOKYO, JAPAN INVITED HIM TO PARTICIPATE IN A RETROSPECTIVE OF HIS WORK AT THE AXIS GALLERY IN TOKYO IN 1982.

PERFORMING ARTIST
THE MOVE
ALBUM TITLE
THE BEST OF THE MOVE
ART DIRECTOR
ROD DYER
ILLUSTRATOR
MICK HAGGERTY
RECORD COMPANY
© A & M RECORDS

PERFORMING ARTIST
MARSHALL HAIN
ALBUM TITLE
DANCING IN THE CITY
DESIGNER
BILL NAGLES
RECORD COMPANY
© EMI RECORDS

PERFORMING ARTIST
THE WHO
ALBUM TITLE
THE WHO TOUR (USA & CANADA 1976)
DESIGNERS
PHILLIP CHIANG AND ROD DYER
ART DIRECTOR
GEORGE OSAKI
RECORD COMPANY
© MCA RECORDS

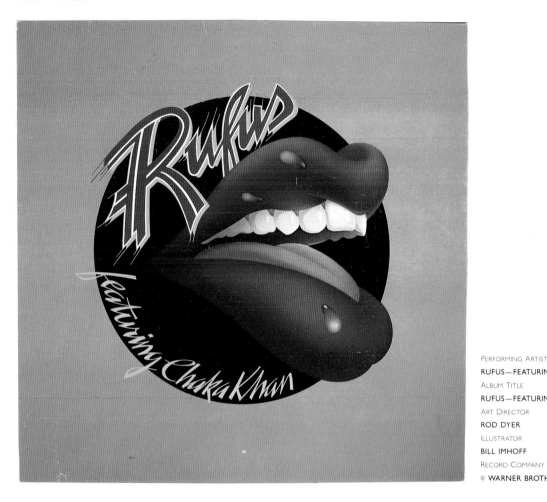

PERFORMING ARTIST
RUFUS—FEATURING CHAKA KHAN
ALBUM TITLE
RUFUS—FEATURING CHAKA KHAN
ART DIRECTOR
ROD DYER
ILLUSTRATOR
BILL IMHOFF
RECORD COMPANY
© **WARNER BROTHERS RECORDS**

PERFORMING ARTIST
AHMAD JAMAL
ALBUM TITLE
AHMAD JAMAL '73
DESIGNER
PHILLIP CHAING
ART DIRECTOR
ROD DYER
RECORD COMPANY
© **WARNER BROTHERS RECORDS**

PERFORMING ARTIST

DIANA ROSS

ALBUM TITLE

AN EVENING WITH DIANA

DESIGNER

RICK SEIREENI

ART DIRECTOR

ROD DYER

RECORD COMPANY

© **MOTOWN RECORDS**

PERFORMING ARTIST

VARIOUS ARTISTS

ALBUM TITLE

THE FORTIES THE FIFTIES

DESIGNER

ROD DYER

ART DIRECTOR

GEORGE OSAKI

ILLUSTRATOR

MICK HAGGERTY

RECORD COMPANY

© **MCA RECORDS**

PERFORMING ARTIST

B.B. KING

ALBUM TITLE

MIDNIGHT BELIEVER (POSTER)

DESIGNER

ROD DYER AND VARTAN

ART DIRECTOR

ROD DYER

RECORD COMPANY

© **ABC RECORDS**

PHOTOGRAPHER

ROD DYER

NICK EGAN

BORN IN LONDON, ENGLAND, NICK EGAN ATTENDED THE WATFORD SCHOOL OF ART. HE DESIGNED FOR THE CLASH, RICHARD HELL AND THE RAMONES, THE DEXY'S MIDNIGHT RUNNERS, BOW WOW WOW AND THE ORIGINAL ARTWORK FOR BANANARAMA. HE ART DIRECTED MALCOLM MCLAREN'S VIDEOS AND ALBUM COVERS.

IN NEW YORK, EGAN WORKED WITH BOB DYLAN, MICK JAGGER, THE NEW YORK DOLLS, IGGY POP, THE PSYCHEDELIC FURS AND TESLA. HE DEVELOPED GRAPHICS, LOGOS AND MARKETING DESIGNS FOR MARC JACOBS (NOW OF PERRY ELLIS).

IN AUSTRALIA, HE ACHIEVED INTERNATIONAL ACCLAIM FOR HIS CAMPAIGN FOR INXS' ALBUM "KICK." HE THEN DESIGNED INXS' ALBUMS "X" AND "LIVE BABY LIVE" AND DIRECTED MUSIC VIDEOS.

EGAN RECENTLY SIGNED ON AS A COMMERCIAL/VIDEO DIRECTOR WITH LIMELIGHT IN LOS ANGELES.

PERFORMING ARTIST
DEEE-LITE
ALBUM TITLE
WORLD CLIQUE
DESIGNERS
NICK EGAN AND TOM BOUMAN
ART DIRECTORS
DAISY AND NICK EGAN
HAND LETTERING
TABOO
RECORD COMPANY
ELEKTRA RECORDS
PHOTOGRAPHER
MICHAEL HALSBAND

© 1990 ELEKTRA RECORDS

PERFORMING ARTIST
INXS
ALBUM TITLE
X
DESIGNERS
NICK EGAN AND TOM BOUMAN
ART DIRECTOR
NICK EGAN
RECORD COMPANY
ATLANTIC RECORDS
PHOTOGRAPHER
MICHAEL HALSBAND

© 1990 INXS

PERFORMING ARTIST
INXS
ALBUM TITLE
X (SPECIAL LIMITED EDITION POP-UP CD)
DESIGNERS
NICK EGAN AND TOM BOUMAN
ART DIRECTOR
NICK EGAN
RECORD COMPANY
ATLANTIC RECORDS
PHOTOGRAPHER
MICHAEL HALSBAND

© 1990 INXS

PERFORMING ARTIST
BELINDA CARLISLE
ALBUM TITLE
LIVE YOUR LIFE BE FREE
DESIGNERS
NICK EGAN AND ERIC ROINESTAD
ART DIRECTOR
NICK EGAN
RECORD COMPANY
MCA RECORDS
PHOTOGRAPHER
GRANT MATTHEWS

© 1991 MCA RECORDS

PERFORMING ARTIST
MALCOLM MCLAREN
ALBUM TITLE
FANS
DESIGNER AND ART DIRECTOR
NICK EGAN
RECORD COMPANY
ISLAND RECORDS
PHOTOGRAPHER
ROBERT ERDMANN

© 1984 ISLAND RECORDS

MALCOLM GARRETT

MALCOLM GARRETT, DESIGN DIRECTOR OF THE UK DESIGN CONSULTANCY ASSORTED IMAGES, STUDIED AT READING UNIVERSITY, 1974–1975 AND AT MANCHESTER POLYTECHNIC, 1975–1978. HE DESIGNED FOR THE BUZZCOCKS, SIMPLE MINDS, CULTURE CLUB AND DURAN DURAN. GARRETT JUDGED THE D&AD ANNUAL AWARDS FROM 1988–1990 AND WAS A MEMBER OF THE D&AD DESIGN SUB-COMMITTEE 1989–1990. HE WAS ALSO THE FIRST EUROPEAN INVITED TO JUDGE THE PRESTIGIOUS 11TH NIPPON GRAPHIC EXHIBITION HOSTED BY PARCO GALLERY IN TOKYO. HE HAS LECTURED AT SEVERAL COLLEGES INCLUDING THE ROYAL COLLEGE OF ART.

IN 1983, HE FORMED A PARTNERSHIP WITH KASPER DE GRAAF, THE FORMER EDITOR OF NEW SOUNDS NEW STYLES MAGAZINE. THEY OPERATE IN THE ART AND ENTERTAINMENT FIELDS.

PERFORMING ARTIST
BEF FEATURING LALAH HATHAWAY
SINGLE TITLE
FAMILY AFFAIR (12" SLEEVE—FRONT)
DESIGNER AND ART DIRECTOR
MALCOLM GARRETT
RECORD COMPANY
TEN RECORDS
PHOTOGRAPHER
KEVIN WESTENBERG

CYBEROPTICS ZAP FACTOR
© 1991 ASSORTED IMAGES

PERFORMING ARTIST
BEF FEATURING GREEN GARTSIDE
SINGLE·TITLE
**I DON'T KNOW WHY I LOVE YOU
(7" SLEEVE—FRONT)**
DESIGNER AND ART DIRECTOR
MALCOLM GARRETT
RECORD COMPANY
TEN RECORDS
PHOTOGRAPHER
KEVIN WESTENBERG

CYBEROPTICS ZAP FACTOR
© 1991 ASSORTED IMAGES

PHOTO: PETER ANDERSON

71

PERFORMING ARTIST
DURAN DURAN
SINGLE TITLE
THE WILD BOYS (7" SLEEVE)
DESIGNER AND ART DIRECTOR
MALCOLM GARRETT

RECORD COMPANY
EMI RECORDS
PHOTOGRAPHER
MIKE OWEN

© 1984 ASSORTED IMAGES

12″ SLEEVE FRONT

PERFORMING ARTIST
DURAN DURAN
SINGLE TITLE
THE REFLEX (12″ PICTURE DISC AND PLASTIC SLEEVE—FRONT)
DESIGNER AND ART DIRECTOR
MALCOLM GARRETT
RECORD COMPANY
EMI RECORDS

© 1983 ASSORTED IMAGES

PERFORMING ARTIST
CULTURE CLUB
ALBUM TITLE
COLOUR BY NUMBERS (12″ PICTURE DISC—FRONT)
DESIGNER AND ART DIRECTOR
MALCOLM GARRETT
RECORD COMPANY
VIRGIN RECORDS

PHOTOGRAPHER
JAMIE MORGAN
STYLIST
RAY PETRI

© 1983 ASSORTED IMAGES

PERFORMING ARTIST
CULTURE CLUB
ALBUM TITLE
FROM LUXURY TO HEARTACHE
DESIGNER AND ART DIRECTOR
MALCOLM GARRETT
RECORD COMPANY
VIRGIN RECORDS

PHOTOGRAPHER
JAMIE MORGAN
STYLIST
RAY PETRI

© 1987 ASSORTED IMAGES

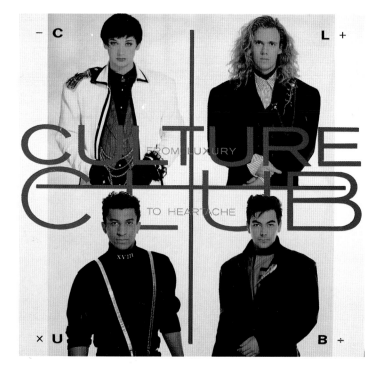

PERFORMING ARTIST
MAGAZINE
ALBUM TITLE
THE CORRECT USE OF SOAP
DESIGNER AND ART DIRECTOR
MALCOLM GARRETT
RECORD COMPANY
VIRGIN RECORDS

© 1980 ASSORTED IMAGES

PERFORMING ARTIST
MAGAZINE
SINGLE TITLE
**A SONG FROM UNDER THE FLOORBOARDS
(7″ SLEEVE FRONT)**
DESIGNER AND ART DIRECTOR
MALCOLM GARRETT

RECORD COMPANY
VIRGIN RECORDS

© 1980 ASSORTED IMAGES

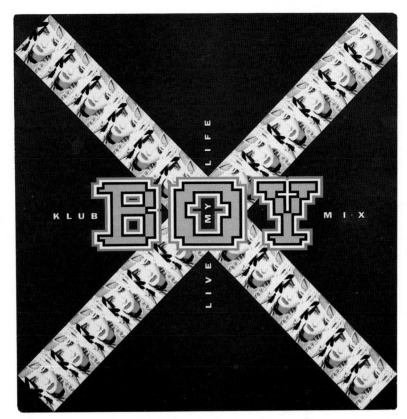

PERFORMING ARTIST
BOY GEORGE
ALBUM TITLE
**LIVE MY LIFE
(12" SLEEVE—FRONT)**
DESIGNER AND ART DIRECTOR
MALCOLM GARRETT
RECORD COMPANY
VIRGIN RECORDS
PHOTOGRAPHER
MARK LEBON

PERFORMING ARTIST
CULTURE CLUB
ALBUM TITLE
THIS TIME (LP SLEEVE)
DESIGNER
MALCOLM GARRETT
RECORD COMPANY
VIRGIN RECORDS
PHOTOGRAPHERS
**MARC LEBON, DAVID LEVINE
AND JAMIE MORGAN**

JEFF GOLD

JEFFREY GOLD IS SENIOR VICE-PRESIDENT OF CREATIVE SERVICES

FOR WARNER BROTHERS RECORDS WHERE HE WORKS ON

PACKAGING, ADVERTISING, MERCHANDISING AND MARKETING OF

THE LABEL'S ACTS. HE HAS ART DIRECTED ALBUM PACKAGES FOR

PRINCE, BRYAN ADAMS, THE NEVILLE BROTHERS, SIMPLE MINDS,

JOHN HIATT AND IN 1990 WON A "BEST ALBUM PACKAGE" GRAMMY

AWARD FOR HIS WORK ON SUZANNE VEGA'S ALBUM "DAYS OF

OPEN HAND."

PERFORMING ARTIST

SUZANNE VEGA

ALBUM TITLE

DAYS OF OPEN HAND

DESIGNER

LEN PELTIER

ART DIRECTORS

JEFF GOLD, LEN PELTIER AND SUZANNE VEGA

RECORD COMPANY

A & M RECORDS

ASSEMBLAGES AND PHOTOGRAPHER

GEOF KERN

COVER CONSTRUCTION AND PHOTOGRAPHER

GEOF KERN

IMAGE OF SUZANNE

GEORGE HOLZ

STYLING PHOTOGRAPHER

DEBRA KERN

PERFORMING ARTIST
ZZ TOP
ALBUM TITLE
RECYCLER (METAL DIGIPAK)
DESIGNER
KIM CHAMPAGNE
ART DIRECTORS
KIM CHAMPAGNE AND JEFF GOLD
ILLUSTRATOR AND LOGO
BARRY JACKSON

RECORD COMPANY
WARNER BROTHERS RECORDS
MEMPHIS PHOTOGRAPHERS
**WALTAIRE "MOJO PHOTO" BALDWIN,
ROBERT "MINT MAN" JOHNSON AND MISS "X" TINE**

© 1990 WARNER BROTHERS RECORDS

PERFORMING ARTIST
SOUND GARDEN
ALBUM TITLE
LOUDER THAN LIVE (PROMO CD)
DESIGNER
LEN PELTIER
ART DIRECTORS
JEFF GOLD AND LEN PELTIER
RECORD COMPANY
A & M RECORDS

© 1989 A & M RECORDS, INC.

PERFORMING ARTIST
38 SPECIAL
ALBUM TITLE
STRENGTH IN NUMBERS
DESIGNER AND ART DIRECTOR
NORMAN MOORE
CREATIVE DIRECTOR
JEFF GOLD
RECORD COMPANY
A & M RECORDS
PHOTOGRAPHER
DENNIS KEELEY

© 1986 A & M RECORDS, INC.

NIGEL GRIERSON

BORN AT FISHBURN, STOCKTON-ON-TEES, CLEVELAND IN 1959, NIGEL GRIERSON RECEIVED HIS B.A. HONS DEGREE IN GRAPHIC DESIGN AT NEWCASTLE POLYTECHNIC, HIS M.A. IN PHOTOGRAPHY AND PHD IN FILM AT THE ROYAL COLLEGE OF ART. HE FORMED 23 ENVELOPE, PHOTOGRAPHY AND DESIGN PARTNERSHIP, WITH VAUGHAN OLIVER PRODUCING RECORD SLEEVES AND POSTERS FOR 4AD. HE DIRECTED THE COMPILATION VIDEO ALBUM "LONELY IS AN EYESORE" FOR 4AD RECORDS, AND HE DIRECTED AND PHOTOGRAPHED VIDEOS FOR BLACK, DAVID SYLVIAN AND CLANNAD. HE CONTINUES TO PRODUCE RECORD SLEEVES AND MUSIC VIDEOS FOR VARIOUS ARTISTS.

HIS WORK HAS APPEARED IN PUBLICATIONS AND IN EXHIBITS IN THE U.S., JAPAN AND EUROPE; HE HAS WON SEVERAL PHOTOGRAPHY AND FILM AWARDS.

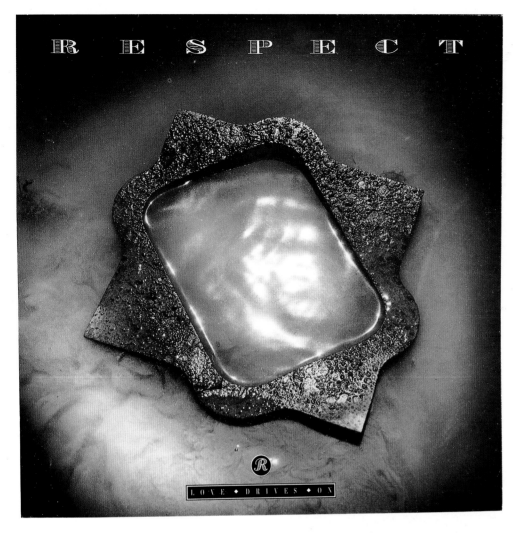

PERFORMING ARTIST
RESPECT
ALBUM TITLE
LOVE DRIVES ON (12" SINGLE)
PHOTOGRAPHER
NIGEL GRIERSON
DESIGNER
VIVID ID
ART DIRECTOR
NIGEL GRIERSON
RECORD COMPANY
CHRYSALIS RECORDS

© 1990 CHRYSALIS RECORDS

PERFORMING ARTIST
THE COCTEAU TWINS
ALBUM TITLE
PEPPERMINT PIG (12" SINGLE)
PHOTOGRAPHER
NIGEL GRIERSON
DESIGNER
VAUGHAN OLIVER
ART DIRECTORS
23 ENVELOPE
TYPOGRAPHY
NIGEL GRIERSON
RECORD COMPANY
4AD

© 1991 4AD

PERFORMING ARTIST
THE COCTEAU TWINS
ALBUM TITLE
ECHOES IN A SHALLOW BAY
(12" SINGLE)
PHOTOGRAPHER
NIGEL GRIERSON
DESIGNER
VAUGHAN OLIVER
ART DIRECTORS
23 ENVELOPE
RECORD COMPANY
4AD

© 1985 4AD

PERFORMING ARTIST
THE COCTEAU TWINS
ALBUM TITLE
VICTORIALAND
PHOTOGRAPHER
NIGEL GRIERSON
DESIGNER
VAUGHAN OLIVER
ART DIRECTORS
23 ENVELOPE
RECORD COMPANY
4AD

© 1986 4AD

BACK COVER

PERFORMING ARTIST
BLACK
ALBUM TITLE
EVERYTHING'S COMING UP ROSES (12" SINGLE)
PHOTOGRAPHER
NIGEL GRIERSON
DESIGNER
JOHN WARWICKER
RECORD COMPANY
A & M RECORDS

© 1987 A & M RECORDS

JERI HEIDEN

BORN IN 1959 IN RED BANK, NEW JERSEY AND MOVED TO CALIFORNIA IN 1969, JERI HEIDEN ATTENDED PEPPERDINE UNIVERSITY AND ART CENTER COLLEGE OF DESIGN. SHE IS CURRENTLY THE VICE-PRESIDENT OF CREATIVE SERVICES/CHIEF ART DIRECTOR AT WARNER BROTHERS RECORDS. SHE SUPERVISES A STAFF OF 12 ART DIRECTORS AND DESIGNERS. SHE HAS BEEN WITH WARNER BROTHERS RECORDS SINCE 1982 AND HAS WON SEVERAL AWARDS INCLUDING 3 GRAMMY NOMINATIONS FOR "ALBUM DESIGN" FOR A-HA—"HUNTING HIGH AND LOW" IN 1986, BRIAN WILSON—"BRIAN WILSON" IN 1988 AND FLEETWOOD MAC— "BEHIND THE MASK" IN 1990. SHE HAS ALSO APPEARED IN ID MAGAZINE, PRINT, ART DIRECTION, THE LOS ANGELES TIMES, MTV MUSIC NEWS AND MANY OTHER PUBLICATIONS.

PERFORMING ARTIST

SHEILA E.

ALBUM TITLE

SEX CYMBAL (CYMBAL CAN)

DESIGNER

SARAJO FRIEDEN

ART DIRECTOR

JERI HEIDEN

RECORD COMPANY

WARNER BROTHERS RECORDS

PHOTOGRAPHER

PHILLIP DIXON

© 1991 WARNER BROTHERS RECORDS INC.

PERFORMING ARTIST

PAUL SIMON

ALBUM TITLE

RHYTHM OF THE SAINTS

PACKAGE DESIGNER AND ART DIRECTOR

JERI HEIDEN

BOOKLET DESIGNER AND ART DIRECTOR

YOLANDA CUOMO

RECORD COMPANY

WARNER BROTHERS RECORDS

BACK COVER PHOTOGRAPHER

BRUNO BARBEY

PHOTOGRAPHY RESEARCH

ESIN ILI GOKNAR

PHOTOGRAPH OF PAUL SIMON

SYLVIA PLACHY

© 1990 PAUL SIMON. WARNER BROTHERS RECORDS, INC.

PERFORMING ARTIST

ELVIS COSTELLO

ALBUM TITLE

SPIKE

DESIGNER AND ART DIRECTOR

JERI HEIDEN

LOGO DESIGNER

JOHN HEIDEN

MODEL MAKING

LIZARD STUDIO

RECORD COMPANY

WARNER BROTHERS RECORDS

PHOTOGRAPHER

BRIAN GRIFFIN

© 1989 WARNER BROTHERS RECORDS, INC. FOR THE U.S.
AND WEA INTERNATIONAL, INC. FOR THE WORLD OUTSIDE THE U.S.

PERFORMING ARTIST
MADONNA
ALBUM TITLE
LIKE A PRAYER (7" SINGLE)
DESIGNER AND ART DIRECTOR
JERI HEIDEN
HAND TINTING
DIANE PAINTER
RECORD COMPANY
SIRE RECORDS
PHOTOGRAPHER
HERB RITTS

© 1989 SIRE RECORDS COMPANY FOR THE U.S.
AND WEA INTERNATIONAL, INC. FOR THE WORLD OUTSIDE THE U.S.

PERFORMING ARTIST
MADONNA
ALBUM TITLE
CHERISH (7" SINGLE)
DESIGNER AND ART DIRECTOR
JERI HEIDEN
RECORD COMPANY
SIRE RECORDS
PHOTOGRAPHER
HERB RITTS

© 1989 SIRE RECORDS COMPANY FOR THE U.S.
AND WEA INTERNATIONAL, INC. FOR THE WORLD OUTSIDE THE U.S.

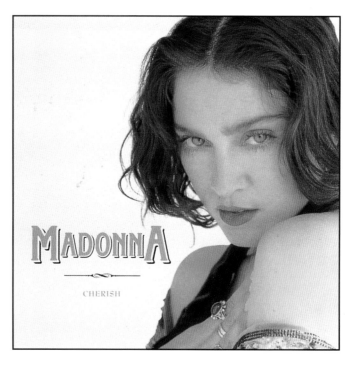

PERFORMING ARTIST
MADONNA
ALBUM TITLE
LIKE A PRAYER
DESIGNER AND ART DIRECTOR
JERI HEIDEN
LOGO DESIGNER
MARGO CHASE
RECORD COMPANY
SIRE RECORDS
PHOTOGRAPHER
HERB RITTS

© 1986 SIRE RECORD COMPANY

PERFORMING ARTIST
MADONNA
ALBUM TITLE
THE IMMACULATE COLLECTION
DESIGNERS
JERI HEIDEN AND JOHN HEIDEN

RECORD COMPANY
SIRE RECORDS
PHOTOGRAPHER
HERB RITTS

© 1990 SIRE RECORDS COMPANY FOR THE U.S.
AND WEA INTERNATIONAL, INC. FOR THE WORLD OUTSIDE OF THE U.S.

PERFORMING ARTIST
MADONNA
ALBUM TITLE
LIKE A PRAYER
DESIGNER AND ART DIRECTOR
JERI HEIDEN
LOGO DESIGNER
MARGO CHASE
RECORD COMPANY
SIRE RECORDS
PHOTOGRAPHER
HERB RITTS

© 1986 SIRE RECORD COMPANY

JIM LADWIG

IN THE YEAR THAT ELVIS PRESLEY HAD HIS FIRST NUMBER ONE HIT, I BEGAN AT MERCURY RECORDS IN CHICAGO, WORKING WITH THE LIKES OF QUINCY JONES, DINAH WASHINGTON, SARAH VAUGHN AND THE PLATTERS. BLIND LUCK!

IN 1968, MY INTEREST IN BOARD PRINTING RESULTED IN THE FORMATION OF AGI WITH DON KOSTERKA AND RICHARD BLOCK. AS CREATIVE DIRECTOR I WORKED WITH DESIGNERS KERIG POPE, DES STROBEL, JOHN CRAIG, DAN CZUBAK, PETER CORRISTON, MIKE DOUD, JOHN KOSH, BOB HEIMALL, JOE KOTLEBA, BASIL PAO, AND BEVERLY PARKER. STARS ALL, DOING SPECTACULAR WORK!

NOW IN THE '90S WITH THE MARVELOUS FORMAT, THE CD, AND AGI'S DEVELOPMENT OF THE DIGIPAK SYSTEM, CREATIVE DIRECTORS ARE ALLOWED UNLIMITED DESIGN OPTIONS. AND...THE BEAT GOES ON!

PERFORMING ARTIST
FACES
ALBUM TITLE
OOH LA LA
ART DIRECTOR
JIM LADWIG
ILLUSTRATOR
JOHN CRAIG
RECORD COMPANY
WARNER BROTHERS RECORDS
PHOTOGRAPHERS
JAK KILBY AND TOM WRIGHT

© 1973 A WARNER BROTHERS RECORD
DISTRIBUTED BY WEA INTERNATIONAL

PERFORMING ARTIST
FUZZBOX
ALBUM TITLE
PINK SUNSHINE
PACKAGE DESIGNERS
SAMANTHA HART AND JIM LADWIG
ART DIRECTOR
ROBERT FISHER
RECORD COMPANY
GEFFEN RECORDS

© 1990 THE DAVID GEFFEN COMPANY

PERFORMING ARTIST
SIOUXSIE & THE BANSHEES
ALBUM TITLE
SUPERSTITION
DESIGNER
JIM LADWIG
ART DIRECTOR
SAMANTHA HART
RECORD COMPANY
GEFFEN RECORDS

© 1991 THE DAVID GEFFEN COMPANY

PERFORMING ARTIST
THE OSCAR PETERSON TRIO
ALBUM TITLE
ELOQUENCE
DESIGNER
DAN CZUBAK
ART DIRECTORS
JIM LADWIG AND DES STROBEL
RECORD COMPANY
MERCURY RECORDS
PHOTOGRAPHERS
JOE ALPER AND CLAUS ORSTED

© 1965 WAYNE PRINTING CORP.

PERFORMING ARTIST
THE ROLLING STONES
ALBUM TITLE
FLASHPOINT
DESIGNER
VODX
PACKAGE DESIGNER
JIM LADWIG
ART DIRECTOR
CAROL CHEN
RECORD COMPANY
SONY MUSIC

THIS COMPILATION © 1991 PROMOTONE B.V.
MANUFACTURED BY COLUMBIA RECORDS, NEW YORK, NY
"ROLLING STONES" AND TONGUE-AND-LIP DESIGN
ARE TRADEMARKS OF MUSIDOR B.V. "COLUMBIA REG.
U.S. PAT. & TM OFF. MARCA REGISTRADA.

PERFORMING ARTIST
DIO
ALBUM TITLE
LOCK UP THE WOLVES
PACKAGE DESIGNER
JIM LADWIG
ART DIRECTOR
JANET LEVINSON
COVER ILLUSTRATOR
WIL REES
RECORD COMPANY
REPRISE RECORDS
PHOTOGRAPHER
MARK "WEISS GUY" WEISS

© 1990 REPRISE RECORDS

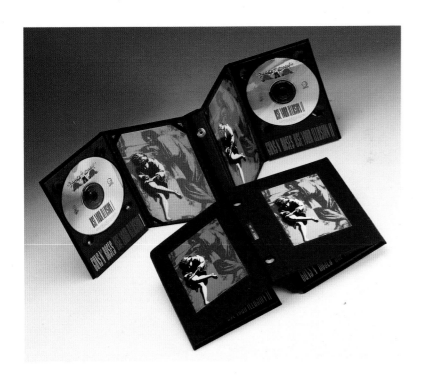

Performing Artist
GUNS N' ROSES
Album Title
USE YOUR ILLUSION I & II
Package Designers
SAMANTHA HART AND JIM LADWIG
Art Director
KEVIN REAGAN
Record Company
GEFFEN RECORDS

© 1991 THE DAVID GEFFEN COMPANY

RANDALL MARTIN

ASSOCIATE ART DIRECTOR, CHRYSALIS RECORDS

RANDALL MARTIN'S FIRST COVER WAS FOR "THE PHANTASMAGORIA," AN ANNUAL FOR HIS JUNIOR HIGH SCHOOL IN THE SAN FERNANDO VALLEY. SINCE THEN, HE ATTENDED NUMEROUS COLLEGES AND RECEIVED THE 1985 SOCIETY OF ILLUSTRATORS SCHOLARSHIP AWARD.

WHILE WORKING AT THE L.A. WEEKLY, HE MET MIKE DOUD, WHO GAVE HIM HIS FIRST ALBUM COVER JOB AND INTRODUCED HIM TO PETER CORRISTON WHEN RANDALL MOVED TO NEW YORK IN 1988.

RANDALL DID A SPECIAL EDITION DIGIPAK FOR BILLY IDOL'S "CHARMED LIFE" ALBUM IN 1990 WHICH HE FEELS GOT HIM HIS CURRENT JOB AT CHRYSALIS RECORDS AS AN ASSOCIATE ART DIRECTOR WITH MARC COZZA.

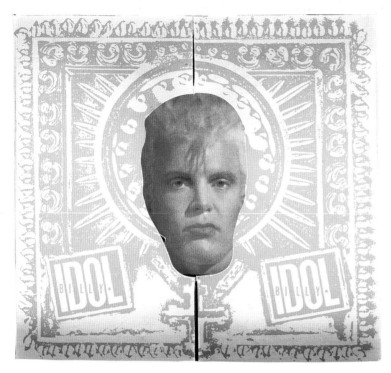

PERFORMING ARTIST
BILLY IDOL
ALBUM TITLE
CHARMED LIFE
DESIGNER
RANDALL MARTIN
ART DIRECTOR
PETER CORRISTON
RECORD COMPANY
CHRYSALIS RECORDS
PHOTOGRAPHER
AGUILERA—HELLWEG (OF BILLY IDOL)
STILL PHOTOGRAPHY
GEORGE KERRIGAN

NORMAN MOORE

BORN IN DUNDEE, SCOTLAND IN 1950, NORMAN MOORE STUDIED GRAPHIC DESIGN AT HARROW SCHOOL OF ART, LONDON FROM 1968–1970 AND AVOIDED GRADUATION TO ACCEPT TWO JOB OFFERS FROM KEN GARLAND ASSOCIATES, LONDON AND IVOR KAMLISH ASSOCIATES, LONDON FROM 1970–1972. HE THEN MOVED TO CALIFORNIA WHERE HE WORKED FOR ROD DYER, INC., LOS ANGELES FROM 1972–1974. IN 1974, HE RETURNED TO LONDON TO OPEN HIS OWN DESIGN STUDIO. IN 1977, HE MOVED BACK TO CALIFORNIA AS ART DIRECTOR AT MCA RECORDS, LOS ANGELES UNTIL HE ESTABLISHED DESIGNART, INC. IN 1979; HIS WORK INCLUDES PACKAGING, MAGAZINES, EDUCATIONAL TOYS AND GAMES, CORPORATE IDENTITIES, ANNUAL REPORTS, CALENDARS, POSTERS FOR FILMS AND MUSIC, BOOK JACKETS AND RECORD COVERS FOR WHICH HE HAS RECEIVED MANY AWARDS INCLUDING THE ART DIRECTORS CLUB OF LOS ANGELES AND NEW YORK, THE AMERICAN INSTITUTE OF GRAPHIC ARTS AND THE DESIGNERS AND ART DIRECTORS ASSOCIATION, LONDON.

PERFORMING ARTIST
GO GOS
ALBUM TITLE
COOL JERK
DESIGNER AND ART DIRECTOR
NORMAN MOORE
RECORD COMPANY
A & M RECORDS

© 1990 I.R.S. INC.

PERFORMING ARTIST   RECORD COMPANY
BELINDA CARLISLE   **VIRGIN RECORDS**
ALBUM TITLE   PHOTOGRAPHER
VISION OF YOU   **KEN NAHOUM**
DESIGNER AND ART DIRECTOR
NORMAN MOORE   © 1988, 1991 VIRGIN RECORDS, LTD.

Performing Artist
HEART
Album Title
BAD ANIMALS
Designer and Art Director
NORMAN MOORE
Record Company
CAPITOL RECORDS

© 1987 CAPITOL RECORDS

Performing Artist
DOWN BY LAW
Album Title
DOWN BY LAW
Designer and Art Director
NORMAN MOORE
Painter
JOY AOKI
Record Company
EPITAPH RECORDS

© 1991 EPITAPH RECORDS

PERFORMING ARTIST
PATRICK O'HEARN
ALBUM TITLE
ELDORADO
DESIGNER AND ART DIRECTOR
NORMAN MOORE

ILLUSTRATOR
NANCY NIMOY
RECORD COMPANY
PRIVATE MUSIC

© 1989 PRIVATE MUSIC

PERFORMING ARTIST
38 SPECIAL
ALBUM TITLE
STRENGTH IN NUMBERS
DESIGNER
NORMAN MOORE
ART DIRECTOR
NORMAN MOORE

RECORD COMPANY
A & M RECORDS

© 1986 A & M RECORDS

PERFORMING ARTIST
PATRICK O'HEARN
ALBUM TITLE
INDIGO
DESIGNER AND ART DIRECTOR
NORMAN MOORE
RECORD COMPANY
PRIVATE MUSIC
PHOTOGRAPHER
THE DOUGLAS BROTHERS

© 1991 PRIVATE MUSIC

ALBUM TITLE
PRIVATE MUSIC SAMPLER 5
DESIGNER AND ART DIRECTOR
NORMAN MOORE
RECORD COMPANY
PRIVATE MUSIC

© 1990 PRIVATE MUSIC

LAURA LIPUMA-NASH

"AFTER GRADUATING FROM OHIO UNIVERSITY IN 1977 WITH A GRAPHIC ARTS MAJOR, MY DREAM JOB WAS TO DESIGN ALBUM COVERS. SINCE L.A. WAS THE ONLY LOGICAL CHOICE OF RESIDENCE FOR SUCH A CAREER, I PACKED MY CHEVY AND MOVED WEST.

"I STARTED BUILDING A PORTFOLIO AND CALLING RECORD COMPANIES FOR INTERVIEWS AND FREELANCE WORK. MY LUCKY DAY CAME WHEN AT THE RIGHT TIME, RIGHT PLACE, I CALLED WARNER BROS. RECORDS AND BASICALLY STARTED MY CAREER IN THE RECORD BUSINESS.

"TEN YEARS LATER I'M STILL WITH WARNER BROS. RECORDS IN A GENTLER, KINDER ENVIRONMENT—NASHVILLE."

PRINCE AND THE R

EVOLUTION / PARADE

PRINCE AND THE R

EVOLUTION / PARADE

PERFORMING ARTIST
PRINCE AND THE REVOLUTION
ALBUM TITLE
PARADE
DESIGNER
LAURA LI PUMA-NASH
ART DIRECTORS
JEFFREY KENT AYEROFF AND LAURA LIPUMA-NASH
RECORD COMPANY
WARNER BROS. RECORDS
PHOTOGRAPHER
JEFF KATZ

MICHAEL•NASH ASSOCIATES

STEPHANIE NASH AND ANTHONY MICHAEL MET AT SAINT MARTINS

SCHOOL OF ART IN LONDON IN 1978 WHERE THEY BOTH STUDIED

GRAPHIC DESIGN. THEY FORMED A PARTNERSHIP CALLED MICHAEL

NASH ASSOCIATES. AFTER LEAVING COLLEGE, STEPHANIE WORKED

FOR ISLAND RECORDS WHILE ANTHONY MICHAEL CO-ORDINATED

THEIR PRIVATE WORK, AND IN 1984, THEY DECIDED TO FORM THEIR

OWN COMPANY.

THEY HAVE DESIGNED NUMEROUS RECORD SLEEVES AND A VARIETY

OF FASHION AND CORPORATE IDENTITY PROJECTS. THEY DO NOT

HAVE A HOUSE STYLE AND APPROACH EACH PROJECT USING

TRADITIONAL VALUES OF GOOD GRAPHIC DESIGN WHICH ENABLES

THEM TO TACKLE ALL AREAS OF MUSIC AND TO PRODUCE UNIQUE

IDENTITIES FOR EACH ARTIST.

PERFORMING ARTIST
RAIN
ALBUM TITLE
TASTE OF RAIN (SINGLE)
DESIGNER
MICHAEL • NASH ASSOCIATES
RECORD COMPANY
© CBS RECORDS
PHOTOGRAPHER
MATTHEW DONALDSON

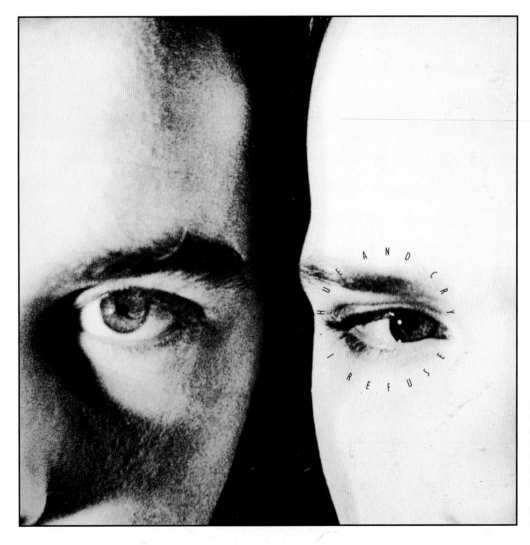

PERFORMING ARTIST
HUE & CRY
ALBUM TITLE
I REFUSE (SINGLE)
DESIGNER
MICHAEL • NASH ASSOCIATES
RECORD COMPANY
© CIRCA RECORDS
PHOTOGRAPHER
ALASTAIR THAIN

PERFORMING ARTIST
MASSIVE ATTACK
ALBUM TITLE
UNFINISHED SYMPATHY
DESIGNER
MICHAEL • NASH ASSOCIATES AND 3D
RECORD COMPANY
© CIRCA RECORDS
PHOTOGRAPHER
MATTHEW DONALDSON

PERFORMING ARTIST
MASSIVE ATTACK
ALBUM TITLE
SAFE FROM HARM (SINGLE)
DESIGNER
MICHAEL • NASH ASSOCIATES AND 3D
RECORD COMPANY
© CIRCA RECORDS
PHOTOGRAPHER
MATTHEW DONALDSON

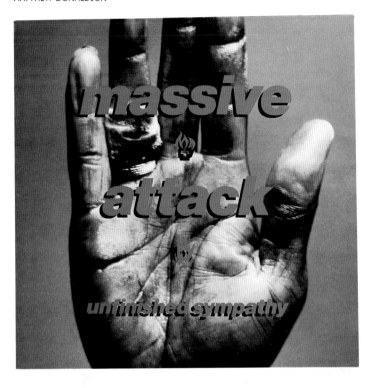

PERFORMING ARTIST
MASSIVE ATTACK
ALBUM TITLE
DAYDREAMING (SINGLE)
DESIGNER
MICHAEL • NASH ASSOCIATES AND 3D
ILLUSTRATOR
DEL NAJA
RECORD COMPANY
© CIRCA RECORDS

PERFORMING ARTIST
MASSIVE ATTACK
ALBUM TITLE
BLUE LINES
DESIGNER
MICHAEL • NASH ASSOCIATES AND 3D
RECORD COMPANY
© CIRCA RECORDS
PHOTOGRAPHER
GRAPHIC

PERFORMING ARTIST
WORLD PARTY
ALBUM TITLE
GOODBYE JUMBO
DESIGNERS
MICHAEL · NASH ASSOCIATES AND KARL WALLINGER
RECORD COMPANY
© CHRYSALIS RECORDS

STYLOROUGE/ROB O'CONNOR

ROB O'CONNOR WORKED AT POLYDOR RECORDS IN LONDON AS DESIGNER/ART DIRECTOR FROM 1979–1981. HE LEFT IN 1981 TO WORK FREELANCE. WITHIN THE FIRST YEAR, HE WAS BUSY ENOUGH TO HIRE MICK LOWE AND THEN NICK WARD. BY 1983, STYLOROUGE (THE NAME CHOSEN FOR THIS VENTURE) MOVED TO LARGER PREMISES. STYLOROUGE WORKED FOR RECORD COMPANIES AND IN THE FILM AND FASHION INDUSTRIES. BY 1984, THE 4 STAFF MEMBERS AT STYLOROUGE WORKED ON RECORD COVERS FOR ADAM ANT, ORANGE JUICE, ALISON MOYET, KILLING JOKE, PAUL YOUNG, AND BOOK DESIGN PROJECTS FOR ROCK BIOGRAPHIES, RAN ALONGSIDE DESIGN FOR RECORD SLEEVES, POSTERS, ADS AND VIDEO COVERS. SINCE 1986, STYLOROUGE MOVED TO LARGER PREMISES AGAIN AND TOOK PART IN SEVERAL EXHIBITIONS IN SCOTLAND, PARIS, ACROSS BRITAIN AND IN LONDON. BY 1991, STYLOROUGE'S 11 STAFF MEMBERS TOOK ON WORK FOR EUROPEAN, AMERICAN AND JAPANESE COMPANIES, AND STYLOROUGE WORKS ON POP VIDEO FOR SEVERAL ARTISTS INCLUDING SQUEEZE, MAXI PRIEST AND ALL ABOUT EVE.

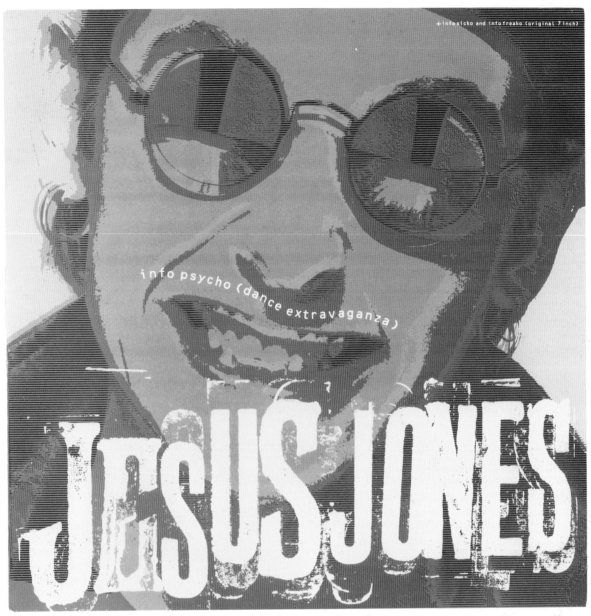

PERFORMING ARTIST
JESUS JONES
ALBUM TITLE
INFO PSYCHO (SINGLE)
DESIGNER AND ART DIRECTOR
STYLOROUGE
RECORD COMPANY
© **FOOD/EMI RECORDS**
PHOTOGRAPHER
SIMON FOWLER

PERFORMING ARTIST
JESUS JONES
ALBUM TITLE
NEVER ENOUGH (SINGLE)
DESIGNER
STYLOROUGE
RECORD COMPANY
© **FOOD/EMI RECORDS**
PHOTOGRAPHER
SIMON FOWLER

PERFORMING ARTIST
GILLAN & GLOVER
ALBUM TITLE
ACCIDENTALLY ON PURPOSE
DESIGNER
STYLOROUGE

ILLUSTRATOR
DAVID DASILVA
RECORD COMPANY
© VIRGIN RECORDS

PERFORMING ARTIST
BLUR
ALBUM TITLE
LEISURE
DESIGNER
STYLOROUGE
RECORD COMPANY
© FOOD/EMI RECORDS

PERFORMING ARTIST
SHRIEKBACK
ALBUM TITLE
BIG NIGHT MUSIC
DESIGNER AND ART DIRECTOR
STYLOROUGE

SCREENPRINTING
KARL SCHOLES
RECORD COMPANY
© ISLAND RECORDS
PHOTOGRAPHER
PETER ASHWORTH

PERFORMING ARTIST
TEARS FOR FEARS
ALBUM TITLE
THE SEEDS OF LOVE
DESIGNER
STYLOROUGE

RECORD COMPANY
© FONTANA
PHOTOGRAPHER
DAVID SCHEINMANN (AVID IMAGES)

UB40
LABOUR
OF LOVE
II

PERFORMING ARTIST
UB40
ALBUM TITLE
LABOUR OF LOVE II
DESIGNER
STYLOROUGE
PAINTING BY
BARRY KAMEN
RECORD COMPANY
© **VIRGIN RECORDS**

UB40 KINGSTON TOWN

PERFORMING ARTIST
UB40
ALBUM TITLE
KINGSTON TOWN (SINGLE)
DESIGNER
STYLOROUGE
PAINTING BY
BARRY KAMEN
RECORD COMPANY
© **VIRGIN RECORDS**

VAUGHAN OLIVER

BORN IN 1957, VAUGHAN OLIVER, BRITISH ART DIRECTOR/DESIGNER AND TYPOGRAPHER, ATTENDED NEWCASTLE POLYTECHNIC, ENGLAND FROM 1976–1979. HE WORKED IN LONDON AS A DESIGNER WITH BENCHMARK AND THEN WITH THE MICHAEL PETERS GROUP. FROM 1981, HE WORKED ON FREELANCE PROJECTS FOR 4AD. HE LEFT THE MICHAEL PETERS GROUP IN 1983 TO WORK FULL-TIME FOR 4AD.

OLIVER AND NIGEL GRIERSON FORMED 23 ENVELOPE, AND AFTER THE DEMISE OF 23 ENVELOPE IN 1988, OLIVER BEGAN OPERATING FREELANCE AND ESTABLISHED V23, WORKING WITH CHRISTOPHER BIGG.

IN 1987, OLIVER CREATED A TOUR-DE-FORCE FOR THE COMPILATION RECORD "LONELY IS AN EYESORE"; HE HAS ALSO PRODUCED BOOK JACKETS, POSTERS, AND TV TITLES.

PERFORMING ARTIST
PIXIES
ALBUM TITLE
VELOURIA
DESIGNER AND ART DIRECTOR
VAUGHAN OLIVER (V23)

RECORD COMPANY
4AD
PHOTOGRAPHER
SIMON LARBALESTIER

© VAUGHAN OLIVER/4AD

BACK COVER

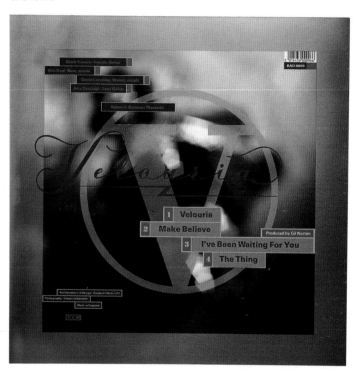

PERFORMING ARTIST
ULTRA VIVID SCENE
ALBUM TITLE
JOY 1967–1990

DESIGNER AND ART DIRECTOR
VAUGHAN OLIVER (V23)
RECORD COMPANY
4AD

© VAUGHAN OLIVER/4AD

PERFORMING ARTIST
ULTRA VIVID SCENE
ALBUM TITLE
STARING AT THE SUN
(BACK COVER)

DESIGNER
VAUGHAN OLIVER (V23)
RECORD COMPANY
4AD

© VAUGHAN OLIVER/4AD

PERFORMING ARTIST
THE BREEDERS
ALBUM TITLE
POD
DESIGNER/ART DIRECTOR
VAUGHAN OLIVER (V23)

RECORD COMPANY
4AD
PHOTOGRAPHER
KEVIN WESTENBERG

© VAUGHAN OLIVER/4AD

PERFORMING ARTIST
LUSH
ALBUM TITLE
BLACK SPRING
DESIGNER/ART DIRECTOR
VAUGHAN OLIVER (V23)

RECORD COMPANY
4AD
PHOTOGRAPHER
JIM FRIEDMAN

© VAUGHAN OLIVER/4AD

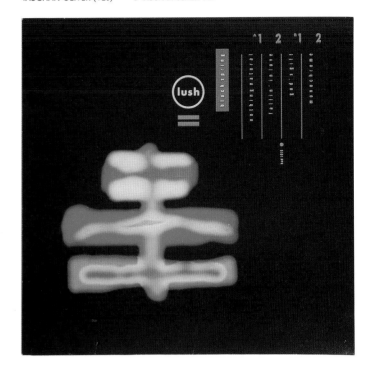

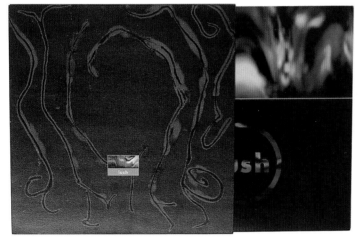

PERFORMING ARTIST
LUSH
ALBUM TITLE
GALA
DESIGNERS
CHRIS BIGG AND VAUGHAN OLIVER (V23)
RECORD COMPANY
4AD
PHOTOGRAPHER
JIM FRIEDMAN

© VAUGHAN OLIVER/4AD

PERFORMING ARTIST
PIXIES
ALBUM TITLE
COME ON PILGRIM
DESIGNER AND ART DIRECTOR
VAUGHAN OLIVER

RECORD COMPANY
4AD
PHOTOGRAPHER
SIMON LARBALESTIER

© VAUGHAN OLIVER/4AD

PERFORMING ARTIST
PIXIES
ALBUM TITLE
TROMPE LE MONDE
DESIGNERS
**CHRIS BIGG, PAUL MCMENAMIN
AND VAUGHAN OLIVER (V23)**

ART DIRECTOR
VAUGHAN OLIVER (V23)
ROCKET ILLUSTRATOR
STEVEN APPLEBY
RECORD COMPANY
4AD
PHOTOGRAPHER
SIMON LARBALESTIER

© VAUGHAN OLIVER/4AD

PERFORMING ARTIST
THE BREEDERS
ALBUM TITLE
POD (POSTER)
DESIGNER/ART DIRECTOR
VAUGHAN OLIVER (V23)
RECORD COMPANY
4AD
PHOTOGRAPHER
KEVIN WESTENBERG

© VAUGHAN OLIVER/4AD

JOHN PASCHE

"BORN AND EDUCATED IN ENGLAND, I MOVED FROM BRIGHTON COLLEGE OF ART IN 1967 TO THE ROYAL COLLEGE OF ART IN LONDON AND COMPLETED MY MASTER'S DEGREE IN GRAPHIC DESIGN. MY FREELANCE DESIGN ACTIVITIES AFTER COLLEGE INCLUDED SEVERAL COMMISSIONS FOR THE ROLLING STONES, INCLUDING THE NOTABLE 'TONGUE' LOGO IN 1971. AFTER A STINT AS AN ART DIRECTOR FOR BENTON & BOWLES AND AS A FREELANCE DESIGNER, I JOINED UNITED ARTISTS RECORDS AS ART DIRECTOR.

IN 1981, I JOINED CHRYSALIS RECORDS AS CREATIVE DIRECTOR WHERE I WORKED UNTIL VERY RECENTLY. WORKING WITHIN THE MUSIC INDUSTRY, I PICKED UP SEVERAL "MUSIC WEEK" AWARDS INCLUDING THOSE FOR TOP POP SLEEVE, TOP CLASSICAL SLEEVE, TOP POINT OF SALE AND BEST TV COMMERCIAL. I HAD WORK PUBLISHED REGULARLY IN THE BRITISH DESIGN AND ART DIRECTORS CLUB ANNUALS. PRESENTLY, I'M SETTING UP A DESIGN COMPANY UNDER MY NAME AND INTEND TO CONTINUE WORKING IN THE MUSIC AND MEDIA INDUSTRIES."

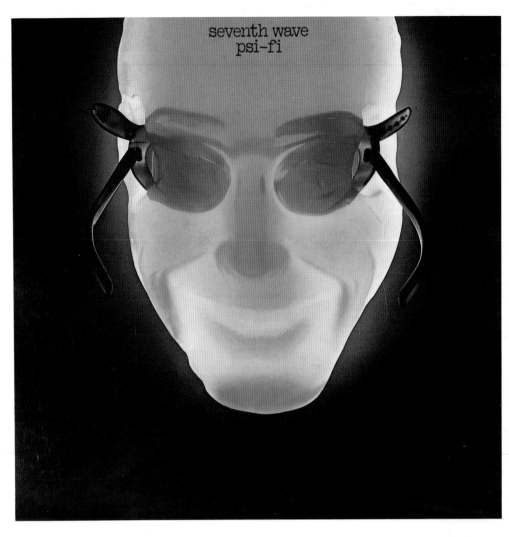

PERFORMING ARTIST
SEVENTH WAVE
ALBUM TITLE
PSI-FI
DESIGNER AND ART DIRECTOR
JOHN PASCHE
RECORD COMPANY
© **GULL RECORDS**
PHOTOGRAPHER
PHIL JUDE

PERFORMING ARTIST
KINGMAKER
ALBUM TITLE
TWO HEADED (EXTENDED PLAY)
DESIGNER AND ART DIRECTOR
JOHN PASCHE
RECORD COMPANY
© **CHRYSALIS RECORDS**

PERFORMING ARTIST
ULTRAVOX
ALBUM TITLE
DANCING WITH TEARS IN MY EYES
DESIGNER AND ART DIRECTOR
JOHN PASCHE
RECORD COMPANY
© CHRYSALIS RECORDS

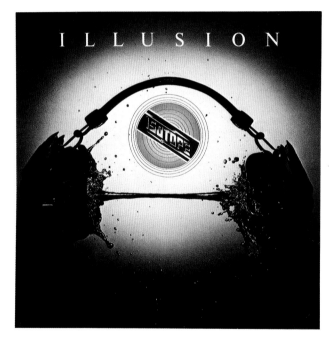

PERFORMING ARTIST
ISOTOPE
ALBUM TITLE
ILLUSION
DESIGNER AND ART DIRECTOR
JOHN PASCHE
RECORD COMPANY
© GULL RECORDS
PHOTOGRAPHER
PHIL JUDE

PERFORMING ARTIST
JETHRO TULL
ALBUM TITLE
STEEL MONKEY
DESIGNER
DAVID ELLIS
ART DIRECTOR
JOHN PASCHE
RECORD COMPANY
© CHRYSALIS RECORDS
PHOTOGRAPHER
PHIL JUDE

PERFORMING ARTIST
THE ART OF NOISE
ALBUM TITLE
IN NO SENSE? NONSENSE!
DESIGNER AND ART DIRECTOR
JOHN PASCHE
RECORD COMPANY
© CHINA RECORDS
PHOTOGRAPHER
ALAN DAVID TU

PERFORMING ARTIST
THE ART OF NOISE
ALBUM TITLE
IN VISIBLE SILENCE
DESIGNER AND ART DIRECTOR
JOHN PASCHE
RECORD COMPANY
© CHINA RECORDS

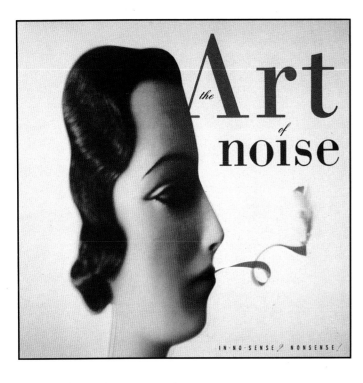

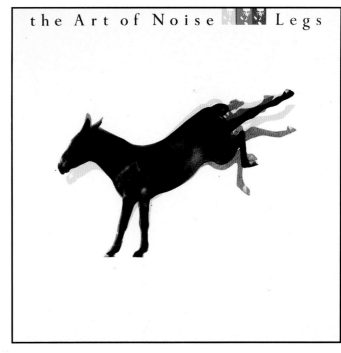

PERFORMING ARTIST
THE ART OF NOISE
ALBUM TITLE
LEGACY (EXTENDED VERSION)
DESIGNER AND ART DIRECTOR
JOHN PASCHE
RECORD COMPANY
© CHINA RECORDS
PHOTOGRAPHER
PHIL JUDE

PERFORMING ARTIST
THE ART OF NOISE
ALBUM TITLE
LEGS
DESIGNER AND ART DIRECTOR
JOHN PASCHE
RECORD COMPANY
© CHINA RECORDS

JANET PERR

JANET PERR MOVED TO NEW YORK CITY IN 1977 AFTER ATTENDING

TYLER SCHOOL OF ART IN PHILADELPHIA. DESIGNING RECORD

COVERS AT CBS RECORDS FROM 1977–1980, SHE WAS INFLUENCED BY

THE MUSIC AND CLUB SCENE OF THE TIME, AS WELL AS NUMEROUS

TRIPS TO OFTEN EXOTIC PLACES. SHE STARTED HER OWN DESIGN

FIRM IN 1982 AFTER A BRIEF STINT AS ASSOCIATE ART DIRECTOR

AT ROLLING STONE MAGAZINE. TWO OF HER LONGTIME GOALS

HAPPENED IN THE '80S—WINNING A GRAMMY AWARD FOR (CYNDI

LAUPER'S "SHE'S SO UNUSUAL") AND WORKING WITH THE ROLLING

STONES. SHE OPERATES HER OWN DESIGN FIRM AND SPLITS HER

TIME BETWEEN RESIDENCES IN NEW YORK CITY AND RURAL

UPSTATE NEW YORK.

PERFORMING ARTIST
CYNDI LAUPER
ALBUM TITLE
SHE BOP (12" SINGLE)
DESIGNER AND ART DIRECTOR
JANET PERR
ILLUSTRATOR
MARK MAREK
RECORD COMPANY
EPIC RECORDS

© 1984 EPIC RECORDS

PERFORMING ARTIST
CYNDI LAUPER
ALBUM TITLE
SHE'S SO UNUSUAL
DESIGNER AND ART DIRECTOR
JANET PERR
RECORD COMPANY
EPIC RECORDS
PHOTOGRAPHER
ANNIE LEIBOVITZ

© 1984 EPIC RECORDS

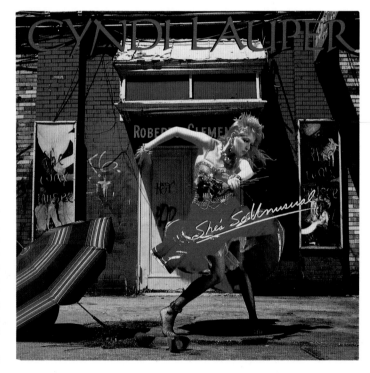

PERFORMING ARTIST
HOOTERS
ALBUM TITLE
ZIG ZAG (1989 KILLED VERSION)
DESIGNER AND ART DIRECTOR
JANET PERR
RECORD COMPANY
COLUMBIA RECORDS

PERFORMING ARTIST
DEVO
ALBUM TITLE
DUTY NOW FOR THE FUTURE
DESIGNER AND ART DIRECTOR
JANET PERR
RECORD COMPANY
WARNER BROTHERS RECORDS

© 1980 WARNER BROTHERS RECORDS

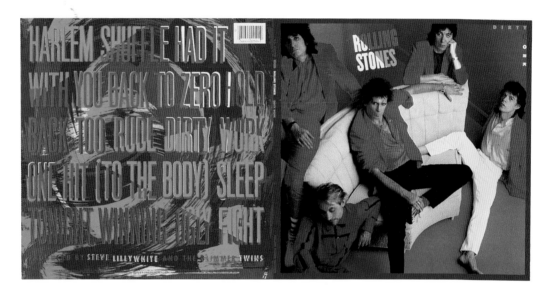

PERFORMING ARTIST
THE ROLLING STONES
ALBUM TITLE
DIRTY WORK (FRONT AND BACK COVERS)
DESIGNER AND ART DIRECTOR
JANET PERR
RECORD COMPANY
ROLLING STONES RECORDS
PHOTOGRAPHER
ANNIE LEIBOVITZ

© 1986 ROLLING STONES RECORDS

PERFORMING ARTIST
FLASH AND THE PAN
ALBUM TITLE
FLASH AND THE PAN
DESIGNERS AND ART DIRECTORS
JANET PERR AND GENE GREIF
RECORD COMPANY
EPIC RECORDS
PHOTOGRAPHER
KEN AMBROSE

© 1980 EPIC RECORDS

PERFORMING ARTIST
RUN-D.M.C.
ALBUM TITLE
RAISING HELL
DESIGNER AND ART DIRECTOR
JANET PERR
RECORD COMPANY
PROFILE RECORDS
PHOTOGRAPHER
CAROLINE GREYSHOCK

© 1988 PROFILE RECORDS

PERFORMING ARTIST
BOB BELDEN—THE MUSIC OF STING
ALBUM TITLE
STRAIGHT TO MY HEART
(1991 KILLED VERSION)
DESIGNER AND ART DIRECTOR
JANET PERR
RECORD COMPANY
BLUE NOTE
PHOTOGRAPHER
MICHELLE CLEMENT

GABRIELLE RAUMBERGER

BORN IN AUSTRIA IN 1951, GABRIELLE RAUMBERGER'S FAMILY MOVED TO LOS ANGELES, CALIFORNIA THE FOLLOWING YEAR. SHE RECEIVED HER BACHELOR'S DEGREE IN ZOOLOGY FROM UCLA AND ENTERED THE ART WORLD AS A BOTANICAL ILLUSTRATOR FOR UCLA AND THE NEW YORK BOTANICAL GARDENS. RETURNING TO LOS ANGELES, GABRIELLE SWITCHED TO ADVERTISING, WORKING AS AN ART DIRECTOR AT MCCANN-ERICKSON. FOUR YEARS LATER, SHE MOVED INTO THE MUSIC INDUSTRY FOR HOGAN ENTERTAINMENT DESIGN, FOLLOWED BY HER OWN DESIGN STUDIO, NEW AGE ART. SHE THEN TOOK A STAFF POSITION AT WARNER BROTHERS RECORDS IN THE MID-80S FOLLOWED BY CREATING AND HEADING-UP AN ART DEPARTMENT FOR GEFFEN RECORDS. SHE IS CURRENTLY WORKING FREELANCE IN THE LOS ANGELES AREA FOR A VARIETY OF CLIENTS BUT STILL SPECIALIZING IN MUSIC ART.

SHE HAS RECEIVED AWARDS FROM THE ART DIRECTORS CLUB OF LOS ANGELES, PRINT REGIONAL DESIGN ANNUAL, THE BELDING AWARD AND AMERICAN AND EUROPEAN ILLUSTRATION ANNUALS, AND A GRAMMY NOMINATION.

PERFORMING ARTIST
BARBRA STREISAND
ALBUM TITLE
JUST FOR THE RECORD...
(CD AND CASSETTE BOX SETS, POSTER,
BOOKLET, COUNTER DISPLAYS AND MERCHANDISING)
DESIGNER AND ART DIRECTOR
GABRIELLE RAUMBERGER
RECORD COMPANY
© COLUMBIA RECORDS
PACKAGING PHOTOGRAPHY
STUART WATSON AND DAVID SKERNICK

GABRIELLE RAUMBERGER

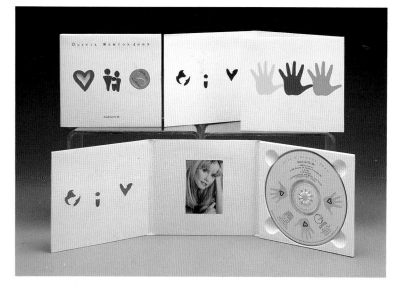

PERFORMING ARTIST
OLIVIA NEWTON-JOHN
ALBUM TITLE
WARM AND TENDER
(SPECIAL CD PACKAGE)
DESIGNER AND LOGO ILLUSTRATOR
LARRY VIGON
ART DIRECTOR
GABRIELLE RAUMBERGER
PACKAGING CONCEPT
JIM LADWIG
RECORD COMPANY
© GEFFEN RECORDS
PHOTOGRAPHER
ALBERTO TOLOT

PERFORMING ARTIST
OLIVIA NEWTON-JOHN
SONG TITLE
REACH OUT FOR ME
(PROMOTIONAL CD PACKAGE)
DESIGNER AND LOGO ILLUSTRATOR
LARRY VIGON
ART DIRECTOR
GABRIELLE RAUMBERGER
RECORD COMPANY
© GEFFEN RECORDS
PHOTOGRAPHER
ALBERTO TOLOT

PERFORMING ARTIST
SHADOWLAND
ALBUM TITLE
GARDEN OF EDEN
(PROMOTIONAL CD WITH ROTATING WHEEL)
DESIGNER, ART DIRECTOR AND LOGO ILLUSTRATOR
GABRIELLE RAUMBERGER
PACKAGING CONCEPT
SAMANTHA MARTINEZ
RECORD COMPANY
© GEFFEN RECORDS
PHOTOGRAPHER
GABRIELLE RAUMBERGER

PERFORMING ARTIST
FRANK ZAPPA
ALBUM TITLE
THEM OR US (LP COVER)
DESIGNER, ART DIRECTOR AND LOGO DESIGNER
GABRIELLE RAUMBERGER
ILLUSTRATOR
DONALD ROLLER WILSON
RECORD COMPANY
© BARKING PUMPKIN RECORDS

PERFORMING ARTIST
BILLY JOE WALKER, JR.
ALBUM TITLE
THE WALK (CD AND CASSETTE PACKAGES)
DESIGNER AND ART DIRECTOR
GABRIELLE RAUMBERGER
RECORD COMPANY
© GEFFEN RECORDS
PHOTOGRAPHER
RON KEITH

PROJECT NAME
**GEFFEN INSTITUTIONAL AD
(CORPORATE AD)**
DESIGNER AND ART DIRECTOR
GABRIELLE RAUMBERGER
ILLUSTRATOR
RAPHAEL GOETHALS
COPYWRITER
JULIE HALL
RECORD COMPANY
© GEFFEN RECORDS

TOM RECCHION

BORN IN 1953 IN MCKEES ROCKS, PENNSYLVANIA AND CURRENTLY AN ART DIRECTOR FOR WARNER BROTHERS RECORDS, TOM RECCHION ATTEND VARIOUS CALIFORNIA COLLEGES INCLUDING PASADENA CITY COLLEGE, EAST LOS ANGELES CITY COLLEGE, MOUNT SAN ANTONIO JUNIOR COLLEGE, ART CENTER OF DESIGN AND OTIS ART INSTITUTE. HE HAS RECEIVED MANY AWARDS— GRAMMY NOMINATION IN 1989 FOR PRINCE'S "BATMAN SOUNDTRACK" AND IN 1990 FOR LOU REED/JOHN CALE'S "SONGS FOR DRELLA," THE 100 SHOW—AMERICAN CENTER FOR DESIGN, CHICAGO 1991, SCREEN PRINTING ASSOCIATION INTERNATIONAL (SPAI) 1991 FOR JANE'S ADDICTION'S "CLASSIC GIRL" AND "BEEN CAUGHT STEALING" CD LABELS, AND ADLA CERTIFICATE OF MERIT. RECCHION HAS ALSO APPEARED IN SEVERAL PUBLICATIONS, AND IN 1991, HIS DESIGNS FOR DAVID LYNCH "INDUSTRIAL SYMPHONY," R.E.M. "OUT OF TIME" AND LOU REED/JOHN CALE "SONGS FOR DRELLA" WERE EXHIBITED IN CREATIVE ARTS WORKSHOP "MUSIC IN PRINT."

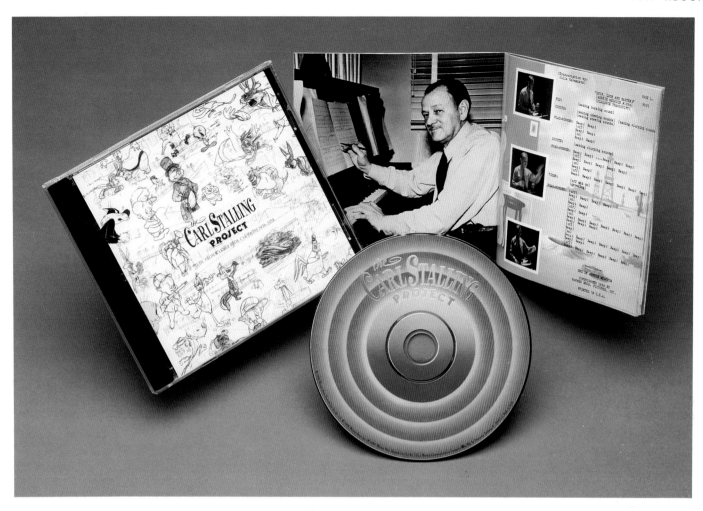

PERFORMING ARTIST
THE CARL STALLING PROJECT
ALBUM TITLE
MUSIC FROM WARNER BROTHERS CARTOONS 1936–1958
DESIGNER AND ART DIRECTOR
TOM RECCHION
ILLUSTRATORS
WARNER BROTHERS ANIMATION ARCHIVES AND STEVE SCHNIEDER ARCHIVES
RECORD COMPANY
WARNER BROTHERS RECORDS
PHOTOGRAPHERS
WARNER BROTHERS ANIMATION ARCHIVES AND STEVE SCHNIEDER ARCHIVES

© 1990 WARNER BROTHERS RECORDS, INC.

PERFORMING ARTIST
VARIOUS ARTISTS
ALBUM TITLE
LASER DISC SAMPLER
DESIGNER AND ART DIRECTOR
TOM RECCHION
RECORD COMPANY
WARNER REPRISE VIDEO
PHOTOGRAPHER
DENNIS KEELEY

© 1991 WARNER BROTHERS RECORDS, INC.

PHOTO CREDIT: DENNIS KEELEY

PERFORMING ARTIST
PRINCE AND THE NEW GENERATION
ALBUM TITLE
DIAMONDS AND PEARLS
DESIGNER
GREG ROSS
ART DIRECTORS
JEFF GOLD AND TOM RECCHION
HOLOGRAM
CHRIS MAHNE, SHARON MCCORMACK AND PETER SORBO
EYE LOGO
STEPHANIE BENNETT
HAIR
EARL JONES
MAKE-UP
KASHA BREUNING AND CHERYL NICK
RECORD COMPANY
WARNER BROTHERS RECORDS
PHOTOGRAPHER
JOEL LARSON

© 1991 WARNER BROTHERS RECORDS, INC.

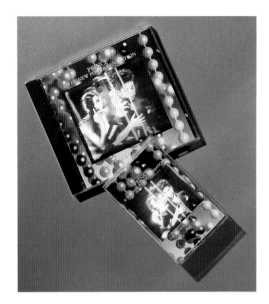

PERFORMING ARTIST

R.E.M.

ALBUM TITLE

OUT OF TIME (LIMITED EDITION CD)

ART DIRECTORS

TOM RECCHION AND MICHAEL STIPE

SINGLE PANELS' ILLUSTRATORS

BEN KATCHOR, TOM RECCHION AND MICHAEL STIPE

HAND LETTERING, SONG TITLES AND R.E.M. LOGO

ED ROGERS

RECORD COMPANY

WARNER BROTHERS RECORDS

PHOTOGRAPHERS

**DAVID GREENBERGER, FRANK OCKENFELS,
ED ROGERS AND DOUG AND MIKE STARN**

© 1991 R.E.M./ATHENS, LTD.

PERFORMING ARTIST
R.E.M.
ALBUM TITLE
LOSING MY RELIGION
ART DIRECTORS
TOM RECCHION AND MICHAEL STIPE
RECORD COMPANY
WARNER BROTHERS RECORDS
PHOTOGRAPHER
ANTON CORBIJN

© 1991
R.E.M./ATHENS, LTD.

PERFORMING ARTIST
JANE'S ADDICTION
ALBUM TITLE
BEEN CAUGHT STEALING (CD SINGLE)
DESIGNER
TOM RECCHION
ART DIRECTORS
JEFF GOLD AND TOM RECCHION
CONCEPT
JEFF GOLD
RECORD COMPANY
WARNER BROTHERS RECORDS

© 1990 WARNER BROTHERS RECORDS, INC.

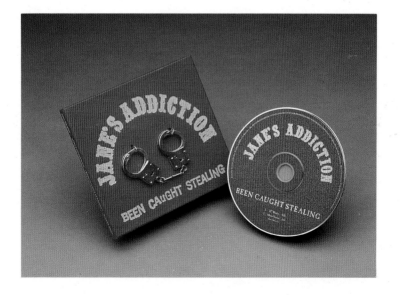

PATRICK ROQUES

PATRICK JOHN ROQUES DESIGNED POSTERS AND 7″ SLEEVES FOR THE UNDERGROUND AND IN 1979 PAINTED THE COVER FOR THE ART-ROCK GROUP TUXEDOMOON'S FIRST ALBUM "HALF-MUTE." THIS COVER WAS AMONG THE "BEST OF THE YEAR" IN VIRGIN'S THE ROCK YEARBOOK 1981. HE CONTINUED TO DESIGN AT POUR-NO-GRAPHICS/RALPH RECORDS.

AFTER LEAVING POUR-NO-GRAPHICS, HE PUBLISHED THE MAGAZINE, "VACATION," AND WAS INVITED TO EUROPE TO BE THE ART DIRECTOR FOR THE BOOK, "A NEW DESIGN FOR LIVING (DESIGN IN BRITISH INTERIORS 1930–1951)." HE DESIGNED SETS FOR THE OPERA "THE GHOST SONATA" IN ITALY, AND FROM 1982–1984, HE LIVED IN BRUSSELS, ART DIRECTING AND DESIGNING ALBUM PACKAGING FOR THE INDEPENDENT LABEL, LES DISQUES DU CREPUSCULE.

IN SAN FRANCISCO HE DESIGNED AN AUDIO CASSETTE/MAGAZINE, "FIFTH COLUMN: PINPOINTS ON A NATION," THEN RELOCATED TO NEW YORK IN 1985 AND SERVED AS ART DIRECTOR FOR "NEW YORK TALK" WHILE ESTABLISHING HIS OWN DESIGN STUDIO, "PRIMARY." HE DESIGNS FOR MANY DIVERSE ARTISTS AND HAS BEEN FEATURED IN MANY INTERNATIONAL PUBLICATIONS.

PERFORMING ARTIST
DEVINE & STATTON
ALBUM TITLE
THE PRINCE OF WALES
DESIGNER AND ART DIRECTOR
PATRICK ROQUES
ILLUSTRATOR
DUNCAN HANNAH
RECORD COMPANY
LES DISQUES DU CREPUSCULE

© 1989 LES DISQUES DU CREPUSCULE

PERFORMING ARTIST
STEVEN BROWN
ALBUM TITLE
HALF OUT
ART DIRECTORS
RAYMOND HALL AND PATRICK ROQUES
RECORD COMPANY
LES DISQUES DU CREPUSCULE
PHOTOGRAPHER
JOSEF ASTOR (PHOTO OF S. BROWN)

© 1991 LES DISQUES DU CREPUSCULE

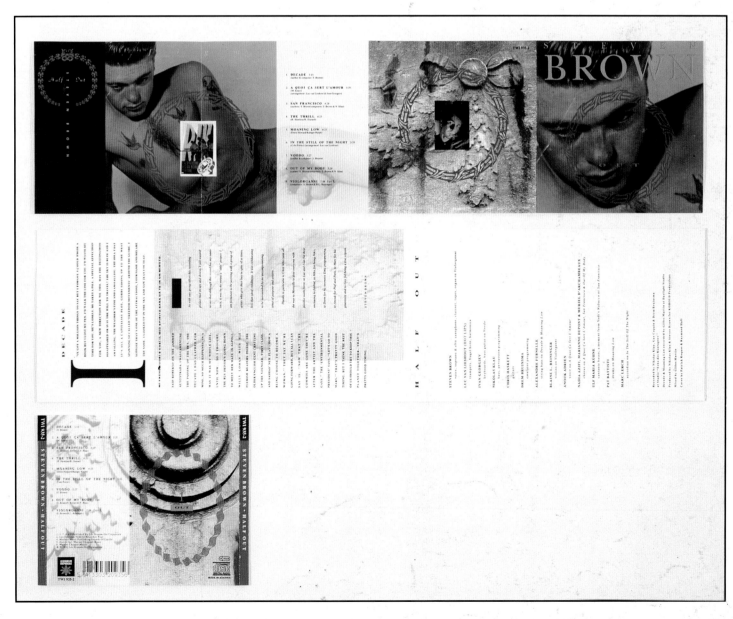

PETER SAVILLE

PETER SAVILLE BEGAN HIS CAREER AS ART DIRECTOR FOR FACTORY RECORDS AFTER GRADUATING FROM MANCHESTER POLYTECHNIC IN 1978. FROM 1979–1983, HE WAS ART DIRECTOR FOR DINDISC, A VIRGIN SUBSIDIARY AND IN 1983, HE FORMED HIS OWN PRACTICE, PETER SAVILLE ASSOCIATES, WITH DESIGNER BRETT WICKENS. IN 1990, HE JOINED PENTAGRAM DESIGN LTD. AS A PARTNER.

PETER'S WORK HAS BEEN THE FOCUS OF EDUCATIONAL THESES, TV AND RADIO DOCUMENTARIES AND PRESS ARTICLES. MANY OF HIS DESIGNS ARE IN THE PERMANENT COLLECTION OF 20TH CENTURY GRAPHIC DESIGN AT THE VICTORIA & ALBERT MUSEUM IN LONDON AND HAS SILVER AWARDS FROM THE ART DIRECTORS CLUB OF PARIS AND THE NEW YORK TYPE DIRECTORS CLUB.

PERFORMING ARTIST

PETER GABRIEL

ALBUM TITLE

SO

DESIGNERS

PETER SAVILLE AND BRETT WICKENS

ART AND CREATIVE DIRECTOR

PETER SAVILLE

RECORD COMPANY

VIRGIN RECORDS

PHOTOGRAPHER

TREVOR KEY

© PETER GABRIEL LTD.

BACK COVER

PERFORMING ARTIST

PETER GABRIEL

SINGLE TITLE

SLEDGE HAMMER (12" COVER)

DESIGNERS

PETER SAVILLE AND BRETT WICKENS

ART AND CREATIVE DIRECTOR

PETER SAVILLE

RECORD COMPANY

CHARISMA RECORDS

PHOTOGRAPHER

TREVOR KEY

© PETER GABRIEL LTD.

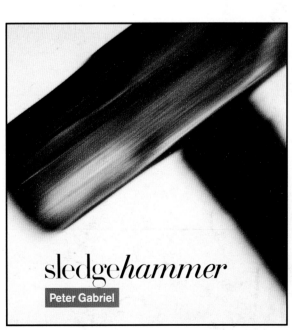

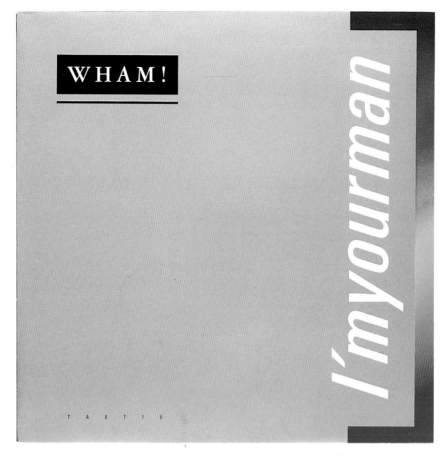

WHAM!

I'm your man

PERFORMING ARTIST
WHAM
SINGLE TITLE
I'M YOUR MAN
DESIGNERS
PETER SAVILLE AND BRETT WICKENS
ART AND CREATIVE DIRECTOR
PETER SAVILLE
RECORD COMPANY
CBS/EPIC RECORDS

PERFORMING ARTIST
NEW ORDER
ALBUM TITLE
POWER, CORRUPTION AND LIES
DESIGNER AND ART DIRECTOR
PETER SAVILLE
PAINTING
FANTIN-LATOUR, COURTESY OF THE NATIONAL GALLERY, LONDON
RECORD COMPANY
FACTORY COMMUNICATIONS LTD.

PERFORMING ARTIST
NEW ORDER
ALBUM TITLE
LOW LIFE
DESIGNER AND ART DIRECTOR
PETER SAVILLE
RECORD COMPANY
FACTORY COMMUNICATIONS LTD.
PHOTOGRAPHER
TREVOR KEY

© 1985 FACTORY COMMUNICATIONS LTD./PETER SAVILLE ASSOCIATES

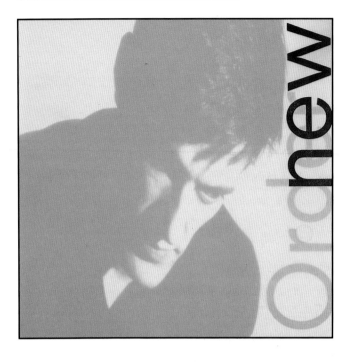

PERFORMING ARTIST
NEW ORDER
ALBUM TITLE
TECHNIQUE
DESIGNERS
PETER SAVILLE AND BRETT WICKENS
ART AND CREATIVE DIRECTOR
PETER SAVILLE
RECORD COMPANY
FACTORY COMMUNICATIONS LTD.
PHOTOGRAPHER
TREVOR KEY

© 1989 FACTORY COMMUNICATIONS LTD./PETER SAVILLE ASSOCIATES

PERFORMING ARTIST
MIDGE URE
ALBUM TITLE
ANSWERS TO NOTHING
DESIGNERS
PETER SAVILLE AND BRETT WICKENS
ART AND CREATIVE DIRECTOR
PETER SAVILLE
CALLIGRAPHER
GEORGES MATHIEU
RECORD COMPANY
CHRYSALIS RECORDS
PHOTOGRAPHER
ROBIN BARTON

© CHRYSALIS RECORDS

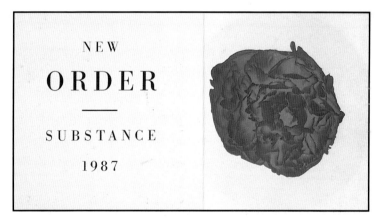

PERFORMING ARTIST
NEW ORDER
ALBUM TITLE
SUBSTANCE
DESIGNER
BRETT WICKENS
ART AND CREATIVE DIRECTOR
PETER SAVILLE
RECORD COMPANY
FACTORY COMMUNICATIONS LTD.
PHOTOGRAPHER
TREVOR KEY

© 1987 FACTORY COMMUNICATIONS LTD./PETER SAVILLE ASSOCIATES

PAULA SCHER

PAULA SCHER BEGAN HER DESIGN CAREER AT CBS RECORDS WHERE SHE DESIGNED RECORD COVERS AND POSTERS. IN 1984, SHE FOUNDED KOPPEL & SCHER WITH TERRY KOPPEL, PRODUCING MAGAZINES, PROMOTIONAL BOOKS AND BROCHURES, PACKAGE DESIGNS, IDENTITY SYSTEMS, BOOKS, BOOK JACKETS AND POSTERS. IN 1991, SHE BECAME A PARTNER OF PENTAGRAM.

SCHER'S DESIGNS HAVE BEEN COLLECTED BY THE MUSEUM OF MODERN ART, THE ZURICH POSTER MUSEUM AND THE CENTRE GEORGES POMPIDOU, AND SHE HAS RECEIVED OVER 300 AWARDS FROM GRAPHIC DESIGN PUBLICATIONS IN THE UNITED STATES. FOR EIGHT YEARS, SCHER HAS TAUGHT A SENIOR PORTFOLIO CLASS AT THE SCHOOL OF VISUAL ARTS AND IS CURRENTLY CO-CHAIRING THE AIGA 1991 NATIONAL CONFERENCE IN CHICAGO WITH PARTNER MICHAEL BIERUT.

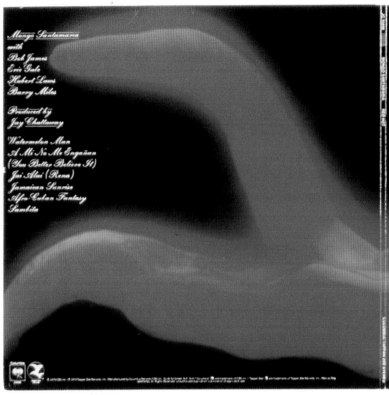
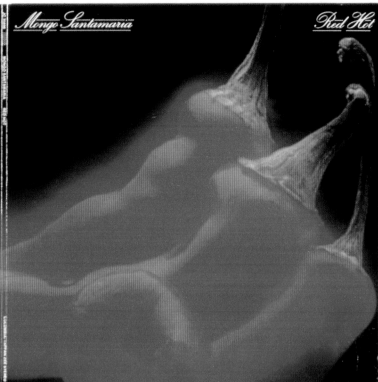

PERFORMING ARTIST
MONGO SANTAMARIA
ALBUM TITLE
RED HOT
DESIGNER
PAULA SCHER
RECORD COMPANY
© RCA RECORDS
PHOTOGRAPHER
JOHN PAUL ENDRES

PERFORMING ARTIST	ILLUSTRATOR
BOB JAMES	**JOHN PAUL ENDRES**
ALBUM TITLE	RECORD COMPANY
HEADS	**© RCA RECORDS**
DESIGNER	PHOTOGRAPHER
PAULA SCHER	**JOHN PAUL ENDRES**

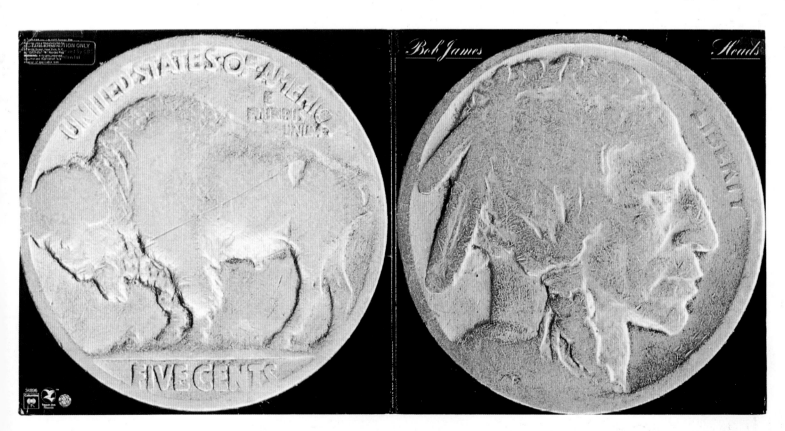

PERFORMING ARTIST
BOB JAMES
ALBUM TITLE
TOUCHDOWN
DESIGNER
PAULA SCHER
RECORD COMPANY
© **RCA RECORDS**
PHOTOGRAPHER
JOHN PAUL ENDRES

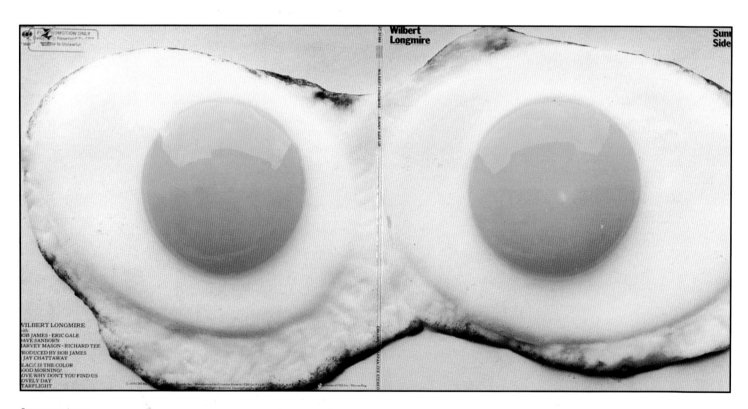

PERFORMING ARTIST
WILBERT LONGMIRE
ALBUM TITLE
SUNNY SIDE UP
DESIGNER
PAULA SCHER
ILLUSTRATOR
JOHN PAUL ENDRES
RECORD COMPANY
© **RCA RECORDS**

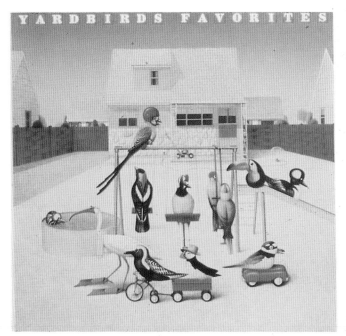

PERFORMING ARTIST
THE YARDBIRDS
ALBUM TITLE
YARDBIRDS FAVORITES
DESIGNER
PAULA SCHER
ILLUSTRATOR
PAUL WILCOX
RECORD COMPANY
© RCA RECORDS

PERFORMING ARTISTS
**BOB JAMES AND EARL KLUGH
WITH RON CARTER, HARVEY MASON,
RALPH MACDONALD, GARY
KING AND NEIL JASON**
ALBUM TITLE
ONE ON ONE
DESIGNER
PAULA SCHER
ILLUSTRATOR
JOHN PAUL ENDRES
RECORD COMPANY
© RCA RECORDS
PHOTOGRAPHER
ARNOLD ROSENBERG

PERFORMING ARTIST
JEAN-PIERRE RAMPAL AND LILY LASKINE
ALBUM TITLE
SAKURA
DESIGNER
PAULA SCHER
RECORD COMPANY
© RCA RECORDS

BILL SMITH STUDIO

BILL SMITH HAS BEEN DESIGNING RECORD SLEEVES SINCE 1976, WHEN HE WAS ART DIRECTOR AT POLYDOR RECORDS. HE HAS WORKED WITH GREAT BANDS SUCH AS THE JAM, THE CURE, GENESIS, QUEEN, AND MORE RECENTLY WITH KATE BUSH, VAN MORRISON, GARY MOORE, LED ZEPPELIN, KING CRIMSON AND MARILLION.

HE SET UP THE BILL SMITH STUDIO IN 1978 AND NOW EMPLOYS SIX PEOPLE. THE STUDIO SPECIALIZES IN DESIGNING RECORD COMPANY WORK BUT ALSO CONVEYS OTHER ASPECTS OF GENERAL COMMERCIAL DESIGN FOR COMPANIES AS DIVERSE AS THE ROYAL SHAKESPEARE COMPANY AND THE INTERNATIONAL AMATEUR ATHLETIC FEDERATION.

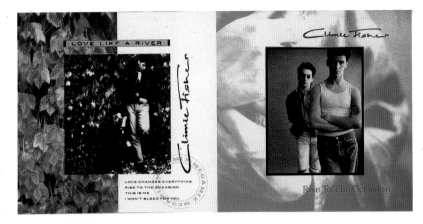

PERFORMING ARTIST
CUMIE FISHER
ALBUM TITLE
LOVE LIKE A RIVER
DESIGNER
BILL SMITH STUDIO
RECORD COMPANY
EMI RECORDS
PHOTOGRAPHER
SARA WILSON

© 1989 EMI RECORDS

PERFORMING ARTIST
CUMIE FISHER
ALBUM TITLE
RISE TO THE OCCASION
DESIGNER
BILL SMITH
RECORD COMPANY
EMI RECORDS
PHOTOGRAPHER
CARRIE BRANOVAN

© 1989 EMI RECORDS

PERFORMING ARTIST
SUNDAY ALL OVER THE WORLD
ALBUM TITLE
KNEELING AT THE SHRINE
DESIGNER AND ART DIRECTOR
BILL SMITH
RECORD COMPANY
VIRGIN EG RECORDS
PHOTOGRAPHER
DOUGLAS BROTHER

© 1990 BILL SMITH STUDIO

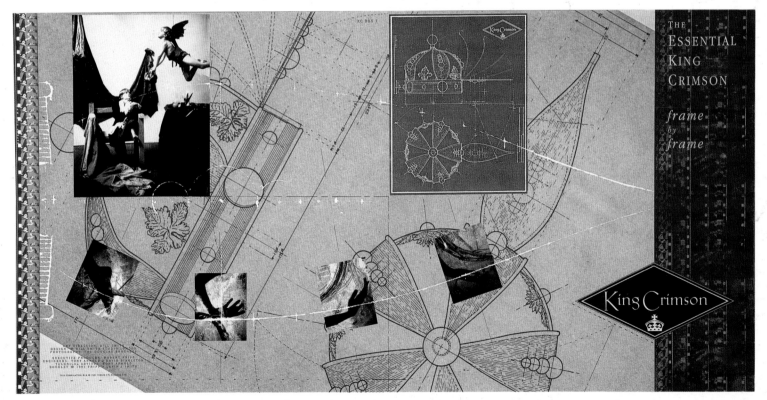

PERFORMING ARTIST
KING CRIMSON
ALBUM TITLE
**THE ESSENTIAL KING CRIMSON: FRAME BY FRAME
(BOOKLET COVER)**
DESIGNER AND ART DIRECTOR
BILL SMITH
ILLUSTRATOR
PETER TRILL

RECORD COMPANY
VIRGIN EG RECORDS
PHOTOGRAPHER
DOUGLAS BROTHERS

© 1991 BILL SMITH STUDIO

TOMMY STEELE

EDUCATED AT THE ART CENTER COLLEGE OF DESIGN AND LOYOLA UNIVERSITY, TOMMY STEELE, VICE-PRESIDENT OF ART & DESIGN AT CAPITOL RECORDS, INC., MANAGES WORLDWIDE ALBUM PACKAGING INVOLVING LP COVERS, DISCS, CASSETTES, SINGLE SLEEVES AND MERCHANDISING AND ADVERTISING CAMPAIGNS FOR SUCH ARTISTS AS TINA TURNER, THE BEACH BOYS, BONNIE RAITT AND BOB SEGER. FROM 1984–1988, HE RAN HIS OWN DESIGN STUDIO, STEELEWORKS WHERE HE DESIGNED FOR TOM PETTY AND THE HEARTBREAKERS, NEIL YOUNG, STEVE MILLER BAND AND SHEENA EASTON. HE IS THE AUTHOR/DESIGNER/PHOTOGRAPHER OF FOUR BEST SELLING POPULAR CULTURE GRAPHICS BOOKS FOR ABBEVILLE PRESS.

FORMERLY, HE WAS ART DIRECTOR/DESIGNER FOR CBS, MCA, ELEKTRA/ASYLUM AND WARNER BROTHERS RECORDS. HE WAS ALSO A FILM GRAPHIC DESIGNER FOR ROBERT ABEL & ASSOCIATES.

PROJECT NAME
PIZZA BOX (CD SAMPLER—STILL LIFE)
ART DIRECTOR
TOMMY STEELE
ILLUSTRATOR
ANDY ENGEL
RECORD COMPANY
© CAPITOL RECORDS
PHOTOGRAPHER
LARRY DUPONT

PERFORMING ARTIST
CROWDED HOUSE
ALBUM TITLE
WOODFACE (SPECIAL EDITION)
DESIGNER
STEPHEN WALKER
ART DIRECTOR
TOMMY STEELE
RECORD COMPANY
© CAPITOL RECORDS
PHOTOGRAPHER
DENNIS KEELEY

PROJECT NAME
PIE BOX (CD SAMPLER)
DESIGNER
JIM HEIMANN
ART DIRECTOR
TOMMY STEELE
RECORD COMPANY
© CAPITOL RECORDS
PHOTOGRAPHER
LARRY DUPONT

PERFORMING ARTIST
TINA TURNER
ALBUM TITLE
FOREIGN AFFAIR (PASSPORT CD)
DESIGNER
GLENN SAKAMOTO
ART DIRECTOR
TOMMY STEELE
ILLUSTRATOR
ANDY ENGEL
RECORD COMPANY
© **CAPITOL RECORDS**

PERFORMING ARTIST
FRANK SINATRA (POSTER)
DESIGNER
ANDY ENGEL
ART DIRECTOR
TOMMY STEELE
RECORD COMPANY
© **CAPITOL RECORDS**
PHOTOGRAPHER
RON SLENZAK

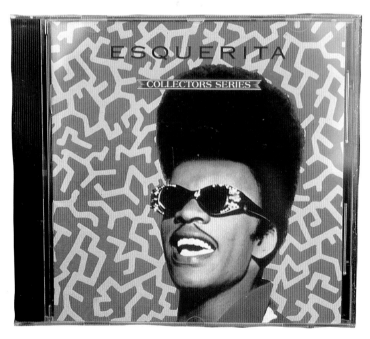

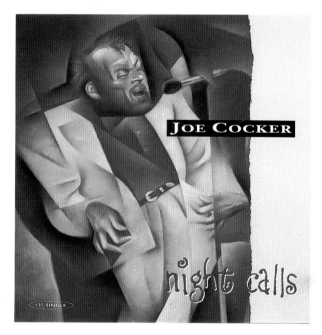

PERFORMING ARTIST
ESQUERITA
ALBUM TITLE
COLLECTOR'S SERIES (CD)
DESIGNER
ANDY ENGEL
ART DIRECTOR
TOMMY STEELE
TINTING
RON LARSON
RECORD COMPANY
© **CAPITOL RECORDS**

PERFORMING ARTIST
JOE COCKER
ALBUM TITLE
NIGHT CALLS
DESIGNER
JOHNNY LEE
ART DIRECTOR
TOMMY STEELE
ILLUSTRATOR
GARY KELLEY
RECORD COMPANY
© **CAPITOL RECORDS**

PERFORMING ARTIST
POINT BLANK
ALBUM TITLE
AMERICAN EXCESS
DESIGNER AND ART DIRECTOR
TOMMY STEELE
RECORD COMPANY
© MCA RECORDS
PHOTOGRAPHER
RON SLENZAK

PERFORMING ARTIST
CHAPTER 8
ALBUM TITLE
FOREVER
ART DIRECTOR
TOMMY STEELE
ILLUSTRATOR
ANDY ENGEL
RECORD COMPANY
© CAPITOL RECORDS

PERFORMING ARTIST
ERIC JOHNSON
ALBUM TITLE
AH VIA MUSICOM (POSTER)
ART DIRECTORS
JEFF FEY AND TOMMY STEELE
RECORD COMPANY
© CAPITOL RECORDS
PHOTOGRAPHER
GEOF KERN

FELIPE TABORDA

FELIPE TABORDA WAS BORN IN BRAZIL IN 1956, GRADUATED FROM THE CATHOLIC UNIVERSITY OF RIO DE JANEIRO AND STUDIED AT THE LONDON INTERNATIONAL FILM SCHOOL IN ENGLAND AND RECEIVED HIS MASTER'S FROM NEW YORK INSTITUTE OF TECHNOLOGY. IN BRAZIL, HE WORKED FOR 4 YEARS AS HEAD OF THE ART DEPARTMENT FOR SIGLA RECORDS AND THEN HEAD OF THE DESIGN DEPARTMENT AT DPZ AND MPM ADVERTISING.

IN 1990, HE STARTED HIS OWN STUDIO, FELIPE TABORDA DESIGN. HE IS CORRESPONDENT TO INTERNATIONAL DESIGN MAGAZINES, AND HIS WORKS WERE SHOWN AT THE BIENNIALS OF POLAND, FINLAND, CZECHOSLOVAKIA, MEXICO AND COLORADO. HIS WORK HAS APPEARED IN SEVERAL PUBLICATIONS, AND CURRENTLY, HE IS ORGANIZING AN EXHIBITION OF 30 INTERNATIONAL GRAPHIC DESIGNERS' WORKS TO BE HELD IN BRAZIL AT THE UNITED NATIONS CONFERENCE ON ENVIRONMENT AND DEVELOPMENT.

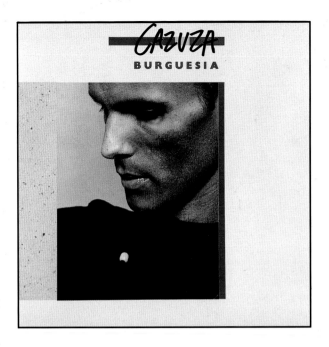

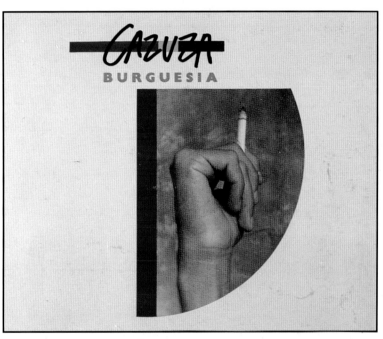

PERFORMING ARTIST
CAZUZA
ALBUM TITLE
BURGUESIA
DESIGNER AND ART DIRECTOR
FELIPE TABORDA
COORDINATOR
ARTHUR FROÉS
RECORD COMPANY
POLYGRAM RECORDS
PHOTOGRAPHER
MARCOS BONISSON

© 1989 POLYGRAM RECORDS

CHRIS THOMPSON

A GRADUATE OF PRATT INSTITUTE IN NEW YORK, CHRIS STARTED AT POLYGRAM RECORDS IN 1987 AS A FREELANCE DESIGNER. CURRENTLY, HE IS ON STAFF AS A SENIOR DESIGNER AND SYSTEMS MANAGER OF THE CREATIVE SERVICE DEPARTMENT'S MACINTOSH COMPUTERS. CHRIS WAS INSTRUMENTAL IN THE CREATION AND IMPLEMENTATION OF POLYGRAM'S STATE-OF-THE-ART COMPUTER SYSTEM WITHIN THEIR DESIGN DEPARTMENT. CURRENTLY, 60 PERCENT OF POLYGRAM'S PACKAGING, ADVERTISING AND MERCHANDISING IS GENERATED ON THE MAC. BETTY CARTER, CRYSTAL WATERS, JOE WILLIAMS, VANESSA WILLIAMS AND XYMOX ARE SOME EXAMPLES OF HIS JOBS CREATED DIGITALLY.

PERFORMING ARTIST
XYMOX
ALBUM TITLE
PHOENIX (POSTER)
DESIGNER
DAVID LAU
ART DIRECTOR
CHRIS THOMPSON
RECORD COMPANY
POLYGRAM RECORDS

© 1991 POLYGRAM RECORDS, INC.

PERFORMING ARTIST
XYMOX
ALBUM TITLE
PHOENIX OF MY HEART (CD SINGLE COVER)
ART DIRECTOR AND COVER ILLUSTRATOR
CHRIS THOMPSON
RECORD COMPANY
POLYGRAM RECORDS

© 1991 POLYGRAM RECORDS, INC.

STORM THORGERSON

STORM THORGERSON WAS BORN IN POTTERS BAR, MIDDLESEX IN 1944 AND EVENTUALLY MOVED TO CAMBRIDGE. HE WAS SCHOOLED AT A.S. NEILL'S SUMMERHILL, BRUNSWICK PRIMARY AND CAMBS HIGH SCHOOL. HE WAS A STUDENT FOR SIX YEARS READING ENGLISH AT LEICESTER UNIVERSITY AND FILM & TV AT THE ROYAL COLLEGE OF ART IN LONDON.

HE BEGAN HIPGNOSIS WITH AUBREY POWELL (PO) IN 1968 AND DESIGNED ALBUM COVERS FOR PINK FLOYD, LED ZEPPLIN, GENESIS, 10CC, PETER GABRIEL, PAUL MCCARTNEY AND MANY OTHERS.

HE TURNED TO VIDEOS IN 1983 BY FORMING GREEN BACK FILMS WITH PO AND PETER CHRISTOPHERSON, AND MAKING CLIPS FOR PAUL YOUNG, YES, ROBERT PLANT, RAINBOW, AND NIK KERSHAW BEFORE DISBANDING IN 1985 DUE TO SEVERE ARTISTIC AND FINANCIAL DIFFICULTIES.

STORM CONTINUED MAKING VIDEOS FOR PMI AND COMMERCIALS FOR HANG FILMS UNTIL 1991 WHEN HE CHANGED COURSE COMPLETELY AND STARTED WRITING SCIENCE FILMS AND ART DOCUMENTARIES.

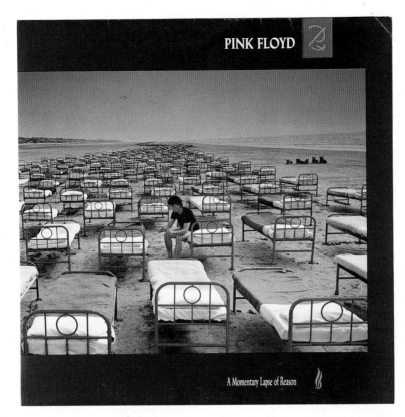

PERFORMING ARTIST
PINK FLOYD
ALBUM TITLE
A MOMENTARY LAPSE OF REASON
DESIGNER
STORM THORGERSON
PHOTOGRAPHER
BOB DOWLING AND TONY MAY
RECORD COMPANY
© **EMI RECORDS**

PERFORMING ARTIST
GODLEY AND CREME
ALBUM TITLE
FREEZE FRAME
DESIGNER/PHOTOGRAPHER
HIPGNOSIS
RECORD COMPANY
© **POLYDOR RECORDS**

STORM THORGERSON

Performing Artist
PINK FLOYD
Album Title
ON THE DARK SIDE OF THE MOON
Designer
HIPGNOSIS
Artwork
GEORGE HARDEE
Record Company
© EMI RECORDS

Performing Artist
PINK FLOYD
Album Title
A COLLECTION OF GREAT DANCE SONGS
Designer/Photographer
HIPGNOSIS

Graphics
NEVILLE BRODY
Photographer
HIPGNOSIS
Record Company
© EMI RECORDS

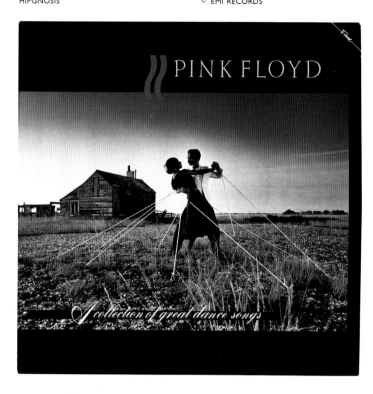

Performing Artist
PINK FLOYD
Album Title
SAUCERFUL OF SECRETS
Designer
HIPGNOSIS
Record Company
© EMI RECORDS

Performing Artist
PINK FLOYD
Album Title
ATOM HEART MOTHER
Designer
HIPGNOSIS AND JOHN BLAKE

Photographer
HIPGNOSIS
Record Company
© EMI RECORDS

PERFORMING ARTIST
MIKE OLDFIELD
ALBUM TITLE
EARTH MOVING
DESIGNER
STORM THORGERSON
RECORD COMPANY
© **VIRGIN RECORDS**
PHOTOGRAPHER
ANDY EARL

LARRY VIGON

"I WAS BORN IN CHICAGO IN 1949. MY FAMILY MOVED TO LOS ANGELES IN 1953, I STARTED ART LESSONS AT AGE 6 AND MAJORED IN ART AT SANTA MONICA HIGH SCHOOL AND SANTA MONICA CITY COLLEGE. AFTER CITY COLLEGE, I ATTENDED THE ART CENTER, COLLEGE OF DESIGN GRADUATING IN 1972. IMMEDIATELY FOLLOWING GRADUATION, I FORMED A DESIGN COMPANY WITH MY BROTHER, THIS PARTNERSHIP LASTED EIGHT YEARS. IN 1980, I BEGAN THE LARRY VIGON STUDIO AND OVER THE PAST TWELVE YEARS HAVE DEVELOPED A SUCCESSFUL AND DIVERSIFIED BUSINESS."

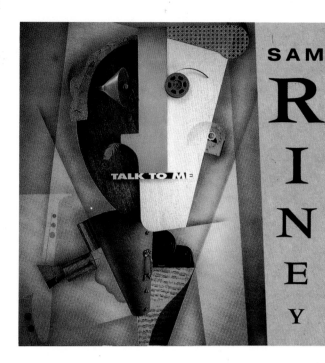

PERFORMING ARTIST
SAM RINEY
ALBUM TITLE
TALK TO ME
DESIGNERS
BRIAN JACKSON AND LARRY VIGON
ART DIRECTOR
LARRY VIGON
RECORD COMPANY
© SPINDLETOP RECORDS
PHOTOGRAPHER
HUGH KRETSCHMER

PERFORMING ARTIST
OINGO BOINGO
ALBUM TITLE
DEAD MAN'S PARTY
DESIGNER AND ART DIRECTOR
LARRY VIGON
RECORD COMPANY
© MCA RECORDS
PHOTOGRAPHER
JAYME ODGERS

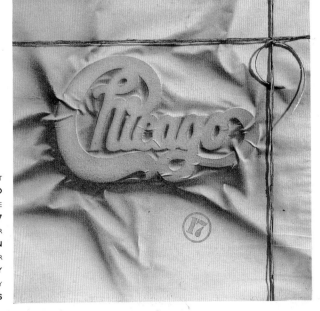

PERFORMING ARTIST
CHICAGO
ALBUM TITLE
CHICAGO 17
DESIGNER AND ILLUSTRATOR
LARRY VIGON
ART DIRECTOR
SIMON LEVY
RECORD COMPANY
© WARNER BROTHERS RECORDS

JOHN WARWICKER

JOHN WARWICKER WAS BORN IN 1955 AND GRADUATED FROM THE CAMBERWELL SCHOOL OF ART WITH A B.A. (HONORS) AND A M.A. (DISTINCTION). FROM 1981–1984, HE WAS AN ART DIRECTOR AT DA GAMA, AND FROM 1985–1988, HE WAS ART DIRECTOR (HEAD OF VIDEO) AT A & M RECORDS INCLUDING 3 MONTHS AT A & M IN CALIFORNIA. FROM 1988–1991, HE WAS THE CREATIVE DIRECTOR AT VIVID, AND SINCE 1991, HE IS CREATIVE DIRECTOR FOR TOMATO, A MULTI-MEDIA CO-OP.

PERFORMING ARTIST
THE ROLLING STONES
ALBUM TITLE
STEEL WHEELS
DESIGNER AND ART DIRECTOR
JOHN WARWICKER
RECORD COMPANY
© **CBS RECORDS**

PERFORMING ARTIST
THE ROLLING STONES
ALBUM TITLE
ROCK IN A HARD PLACE (12" SINGLE)
DESIGNER AND ART DIRECTOR
JOHN WARWICKER
RECORD COMPANY
© **CBS RECORDS**

155

PERFORMING ARTIST
IGGY POP
ALBUM TITLE
REAL WILD CHILD (12" SINGLE)
DESIGNER AND ART DIRECTOR
JOHN WARWICKER
RECORD COMPANY
© A & M RECORDS
PHOTOGRAPHER
ROBERT ERDMANN

PERFORMING ARTIST
SHRIEKBACK
ALBUM TITLE
NEMESIS (12" SINGLE)
DESIGNER AND ART DIRECTOR
JOHN WARWICKER
RECORD COMPANY
© ARISTA RECORDS
PHOTOGRAPHER
NICK KNIGHT

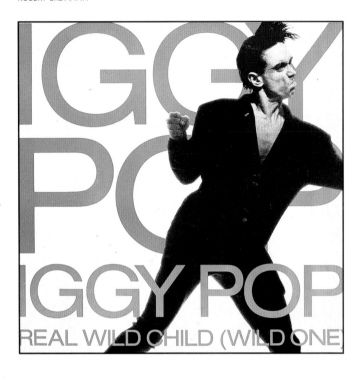

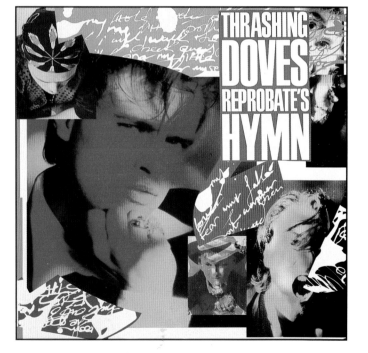

PERFORMING ARTIST
WOP BOP TORLEDO
ALBUM TITLE
WOP BOP TORLEDO
DESIGNER AND ART DIRECTOR
JOHN WARWICKER
RECORD COMPANY
© TEN RECORDS
PHOTOGRAPHER
SATOSHI SAKUSA

PERFORMING ARTIST
THRASHING DOVES
ALBUM TITLE
REPROBATE'S HYMN (12" SINGLE)
DESIGNER AND ART DIRECTOR
JOHN WARWICKER
RECORD COMPANY
© A & M RECORDS
PHOTOGRAPHER
ENRIQUE BADULESCU

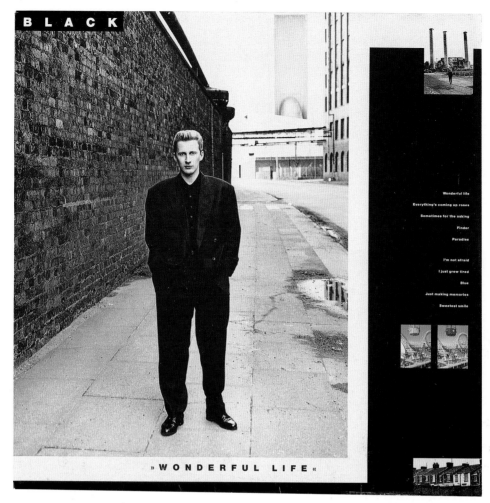

PERFORMING ARTIST
BLACK
ALBUM TITLE
WONDERFUL LIFE
DESIGNER AND ART DIRECTOR
JOHN WARWICKER
RECORD COMPANY
© A & M RECORDS
PHOTOGRAPHER
PERRY OGDEN

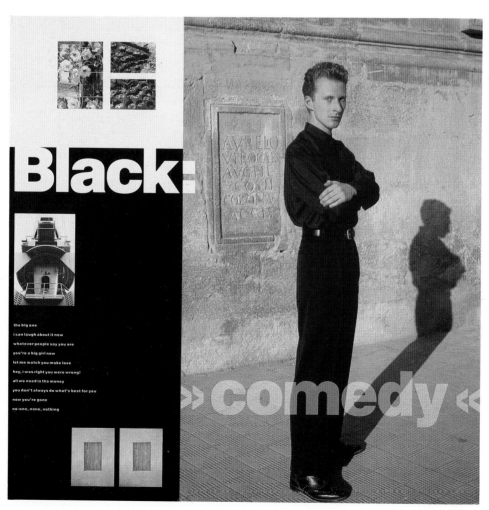

PERFORMING ARTIST
BLACK
ALBUM TITLE
COMEDY
DESIGNER AND ART DIRECTOR
JOHN WARWICKER
RECORD COMPANY
© A & M RECORDS
PHOTOGRAPHER
PERRY OGDEN

TONY WRIGHT

BORN IN LONDON IN 1949, TONY WRIGHT ATTENDED THE CHELSEA ART SCHOOL IN LONDON FROM 1966–1969. IN 1969, HIS FIRST ALBUM COVER WAS COMMISSIONED. IN 1970, HE DESIGNED AN AWARD-WINNING ALBUM COVER "LOW SPARK OF HIGH HEELED BOYS," TRAFFIC. FROM 1970–1980, HE WORKED AS AN ILLUSTRATOR, AND IN 1980, HE MOVED TO AMERICA; HE WAS A CREATIVE DIRECTOR FOR ISLAND RECORDS IN NEW YORK FROM 1980–1990. IN 1991, HE STARTED TWO COMPANIES—"RECORD ART," AN ART PUBLISHING COMPANY, AND "BROKEN GLASS," A BOOK PUBLISHING COMPANY WHOSE FIRST RELEASE, HIS OWN BOOK "HYMN OF THE SUN" WON THE BENJAMIN FRANKLIN AWARD AND THE CATHOLIC PRESS ASSOCIATION BOOK AWARD. HE IS CURRENTLY LIVING IN UPSTATE NEW YORK WITH HIS WIFE AND TWO SONS.

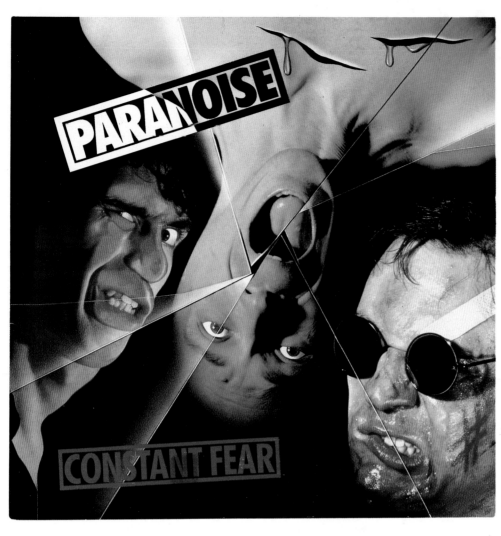

PERFORMING ARTIST
PARANOISE
ALBUM TITLE
CONSTANT FEAR
DESIGNER
TONY WRIGHT
RECORD COMPANY
ISLAND RECORDS
PHOTOGRAPHER
GEORGE DUBOSE

© 1989 ISLAND RECORDS

PERFORMING ARTIST
THE B-52'S
ALBUM TITLE
THE B-52'S
DESIGNER
TONY WRIGHT
RECORD COMPANY
ISLAND RECORDS
PHOTOGRAPHER
GEORGE DUBOSE

© 1980 ISLAND RECORDS

TONY WRIGHT

PERFORMING ARTIST
SLY & ROBBIE
ALBUM TITLE
RHYTHM KILLERS
DESIGNER
TONY WRIGHT
RECORD COMPANY
ISLAND RECORDS

© 1987 ISLAND RECORDS

PERFORMING ARTIST
MARIANNE FAITHFULL
ALBUM TITLE
A CHILDS ADVENTURE
DESIGNER
TONY WRIGHT
RECORD COMPANY
ISLAND RECORDS

© 1982 ISLAND RECORDS